nyc

jacob vendramin

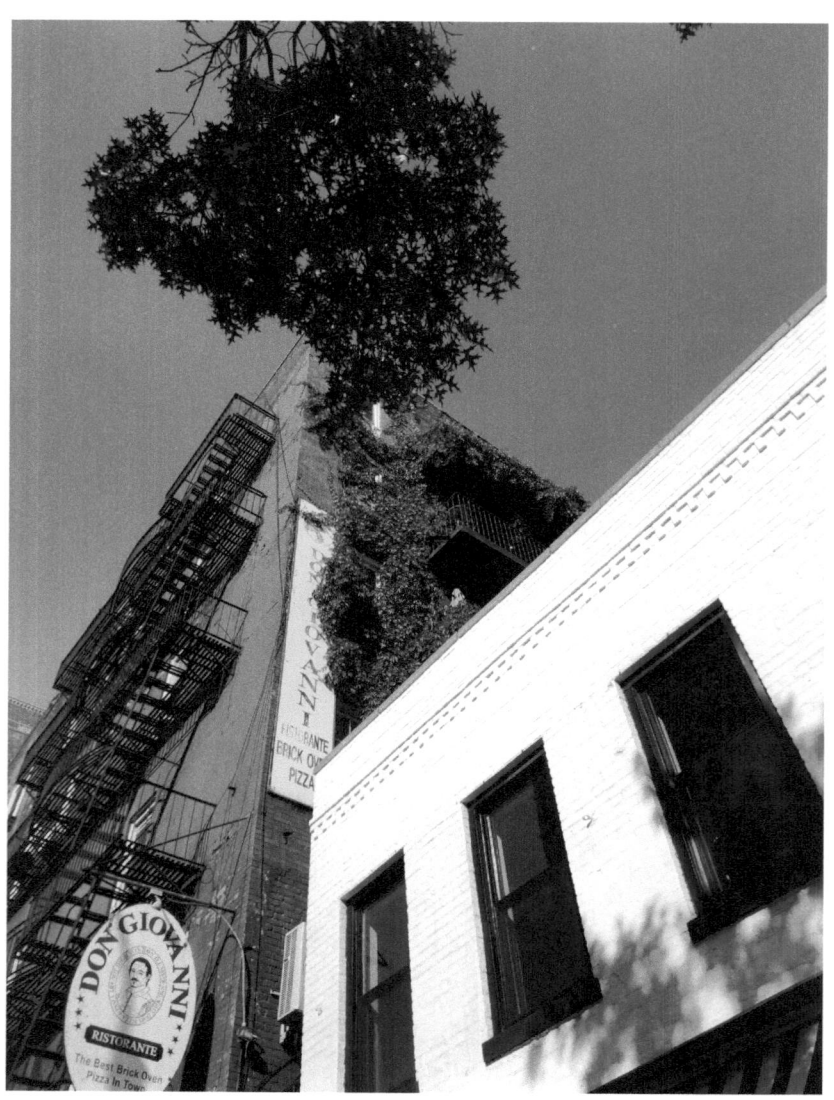

File Name: IMG_20180719_172447.jpg
Date: 07/19/2018 05:24 PM
Width: 3464 pixels
Height: 4618 pixels
Exposure Time: 1/4000 sec.
F-stop: f/1.6
ISO: 50
Focal Length: 27mm
GPS Longitude: West
GPS Longitude: -74.004920959444
GPS Latitude: North
GPS Latitude: 40.747272491389

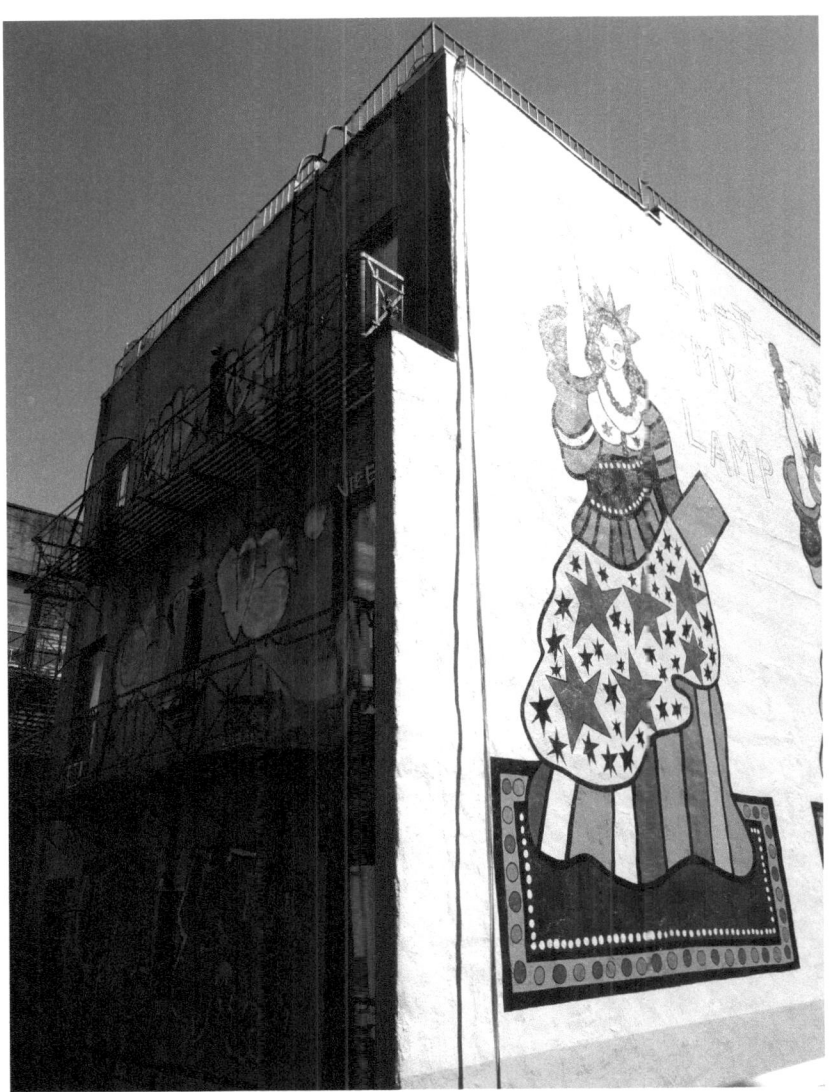

File Name: IMG_20180719_161849.jpg
Date: 07/19/2018 04:18 PM
Width: 3464 pixels
Height: 4618 pixels
Exposure Time: 1/4000 sec.
F-stop: f/1.6
ISO: 50
Focal Length: 27mm
GPS Longitude: West
GPS Longitude: -74.005035400278
GPS Latitude: North
GPS Latitude: 40.747657775833

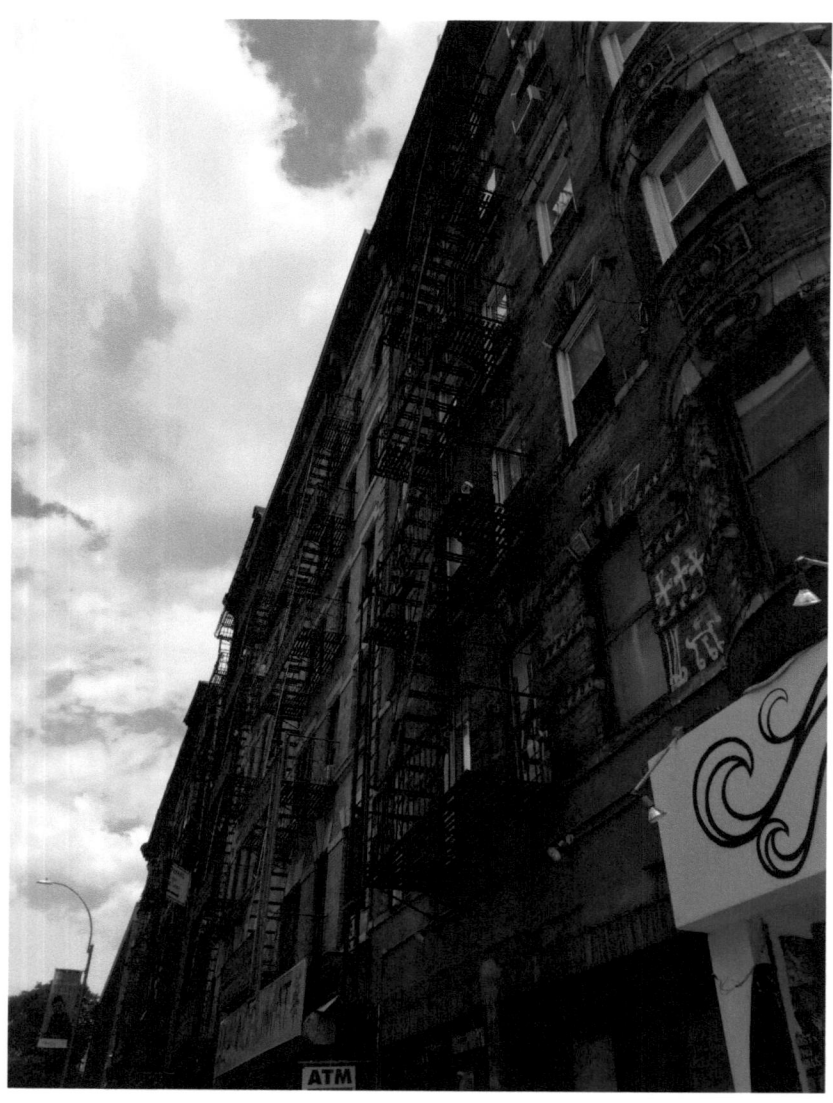

File Name: IMG_20180721_123915.jpg
Date: 07/21/2018 12:39 PM
Width: 3464 pixels
Height: 4618 pixels
Exposure Time: 1/4000 sec.
F-stop: f/1.6
ISO: 50
Focal Length: 27mm
GPS Longitude: West
GPS Longitude: -73.995887756111
GPS Latitude: North
GPS Latitude: 40.720989227222

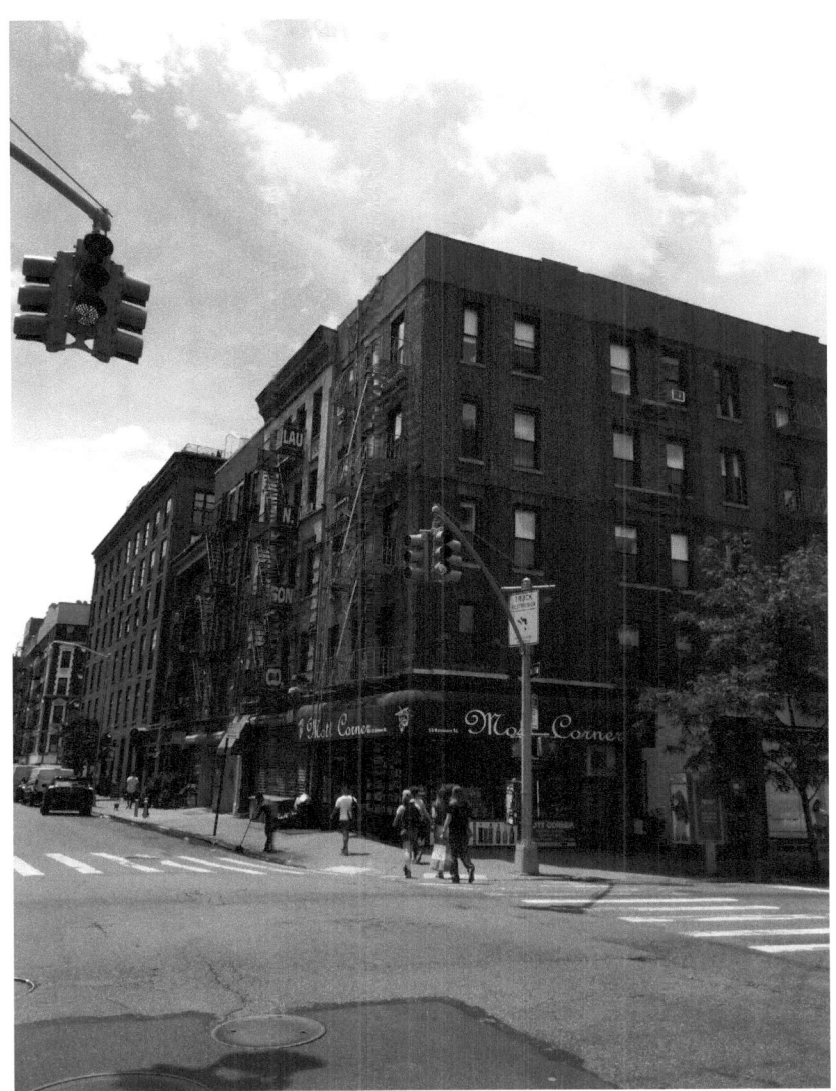

File Name: IMG_20180721_123921.jpg
Date: 07/21/2018 12:39 PM
Width: 3464 pixels
Height: 4618 pixels
Exposure Time: 1/4000 sec.
F-stop: f/1.6
ISO: 50
Focal Length: 27mm
GPS Longitude: West
GPS Longitude: -73.995887756111
GPS Latitude: North
GPS Latitude: 40.720989227222

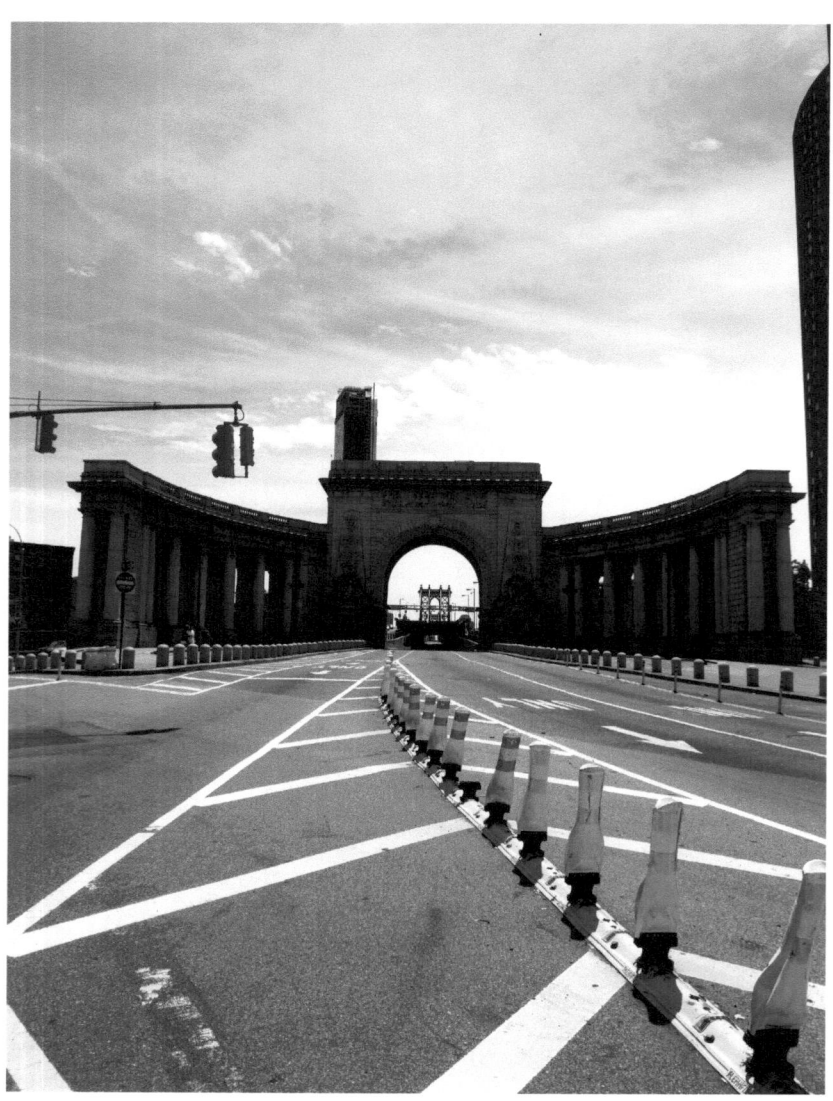

File Name: IMG_20180721_125701.jpg
Date: 07/21/2018 12:57 PM
Width: 3464 pixels
Height: 4618 pixels
Exposure Time: 1/4000 sec.
F-stop: f/1.6
ISO: 50
Focal Length: 27mm
GPS Longitude: West
GPS Longitude: -73.995765685833
GPS Latitude: North
GPS Latitude: 40.716186523333

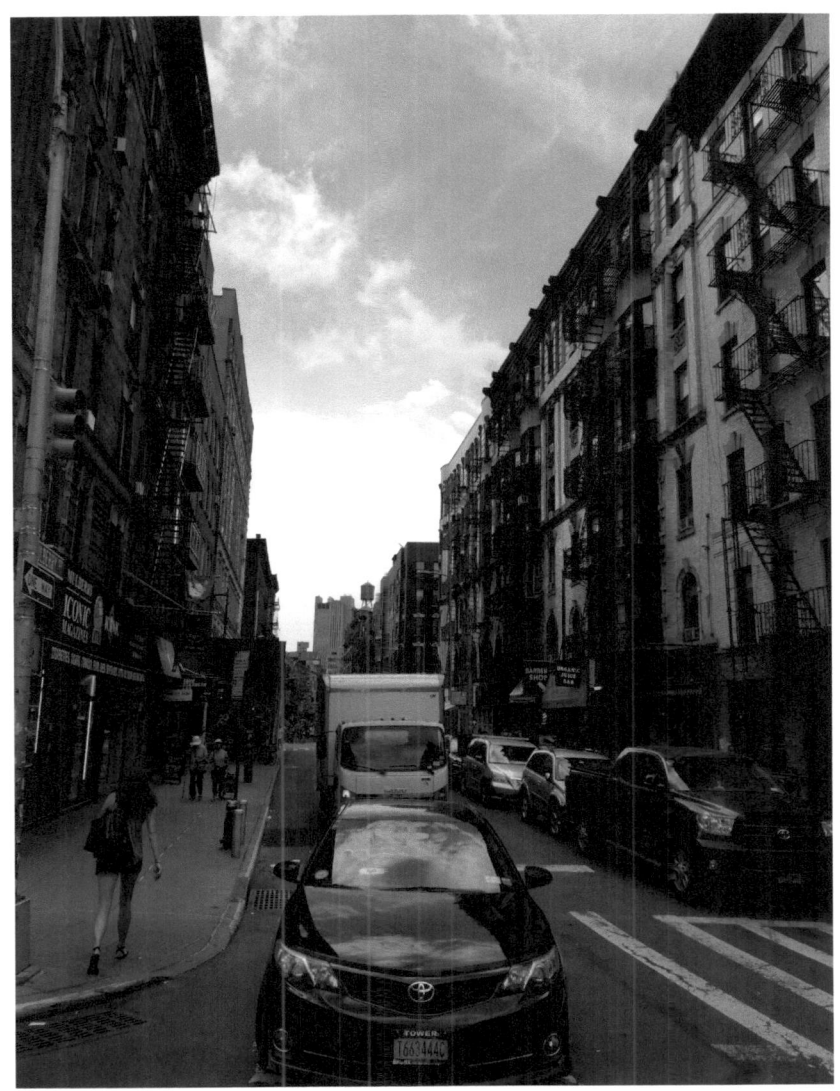

File Name: IMG_20180721_124053.jpg
Date: 07/21/2018 12:40 PM
Width: 3464 pixels
Height: 4618 pixels
Exposure Time: 1/4000 sec.
F-stop: f/1.6
ISO: 50
Focal Length: 27mm
GPS Longitude: West
GPS Longitude: -73.996620178056
GPS Latitude: North
GPS Latitude: 40.721138000278

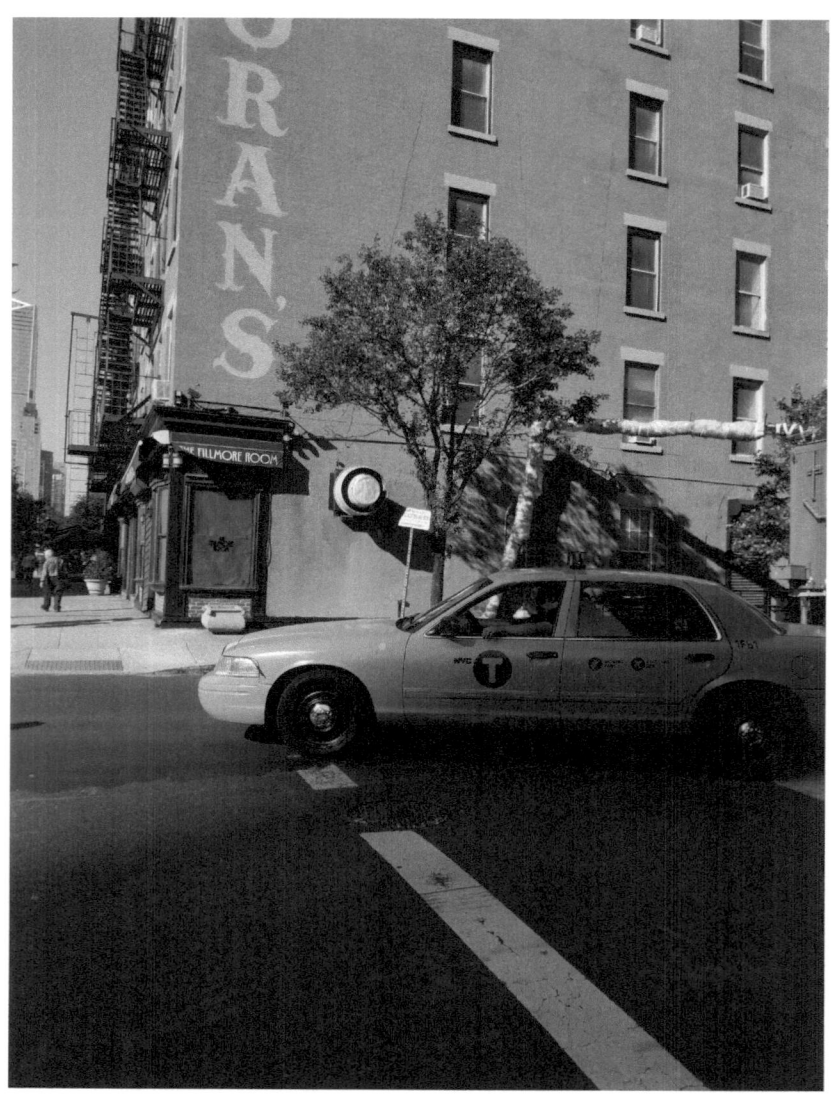

File Name: IMG_20180719_172044.jpg
Date: 07/19/2018 05:20 PM
Width: 3464 pixels
Height: 4618 pixels
Exposure Time: 1/4000 sec.
F-stop: f/1.6
ISO: 50
Focal Length: 27mm
GPS Longitude: West
GPS Longitude: -74.005813598611
GPS Latitude: North
GPS Latitude: 40.745193481389

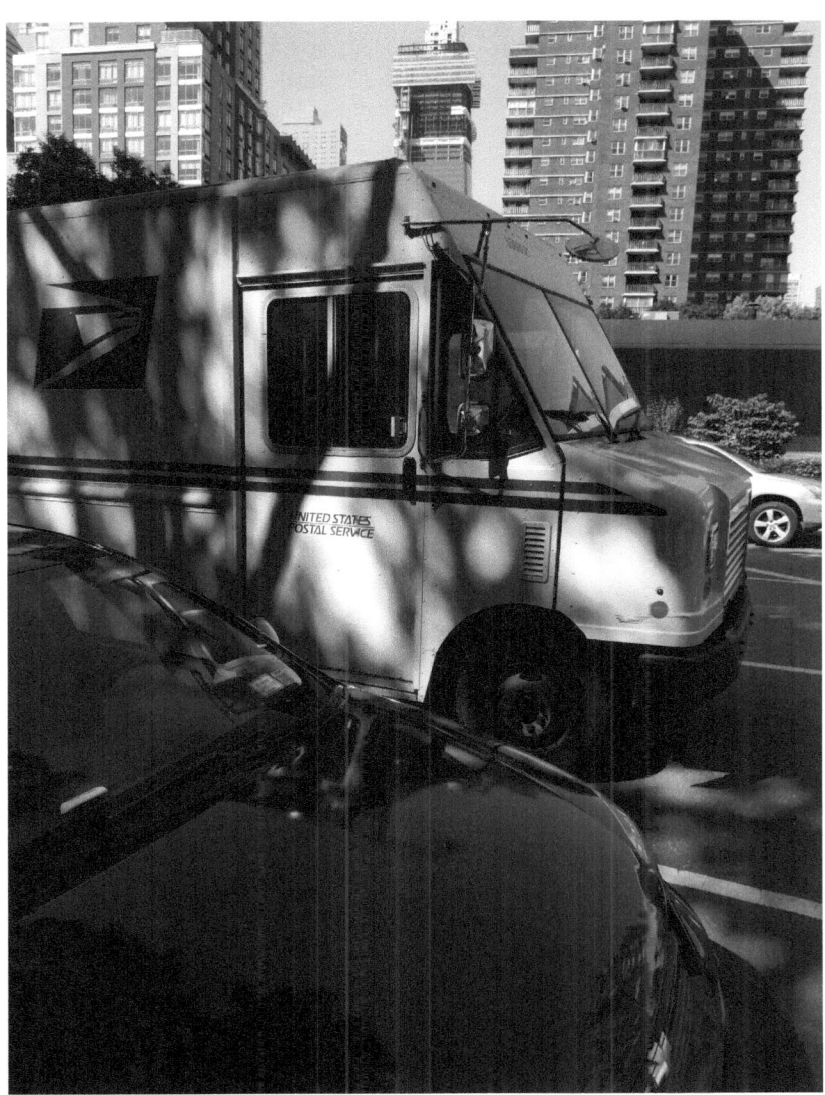

File Name: IMG_20180719_160835.jpg
Date: 07/19/2018 04:08 PM
Width: 3464 pixels
Height: 4618 pixels
Exposure Time: 1/4000 sec.
F-stop: f/1.6
ISO: 100
Focal Length: 27mm
GPS Longitude: West
GPS Longitude: -74.000717163056
GPS Latitude: North
GPS Latitude: 40.747039794722

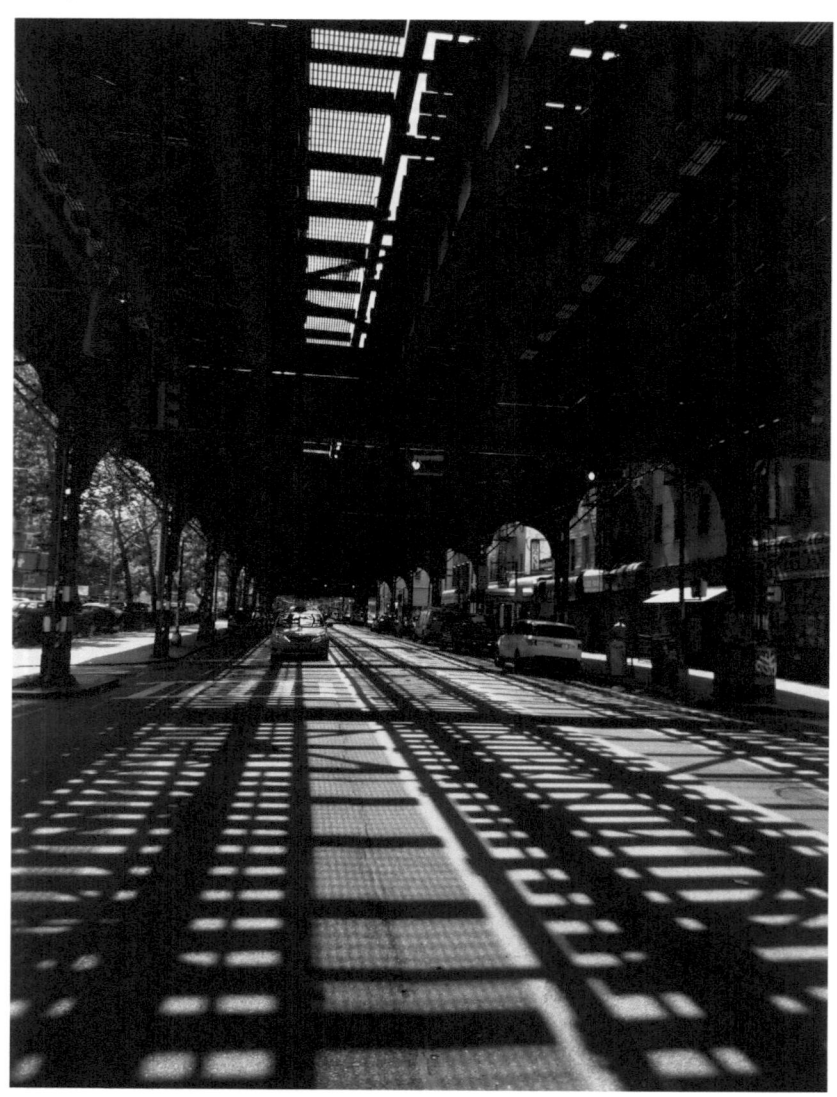

File Name: IMG_20180721_111130.jpg
Date: 07/21/2018 11:11 AM
Width: 3464 pixels
Height: 4618 pixels
Exposure Time: 1/4000 sec.
F-stop: f/1.6
ISO: 50
Focal Length: 27mm
GPS Longitude: West
GPS Longitude: -73.987976074218
GPS Latitude: North
GPS Latitude: 40.689609527587

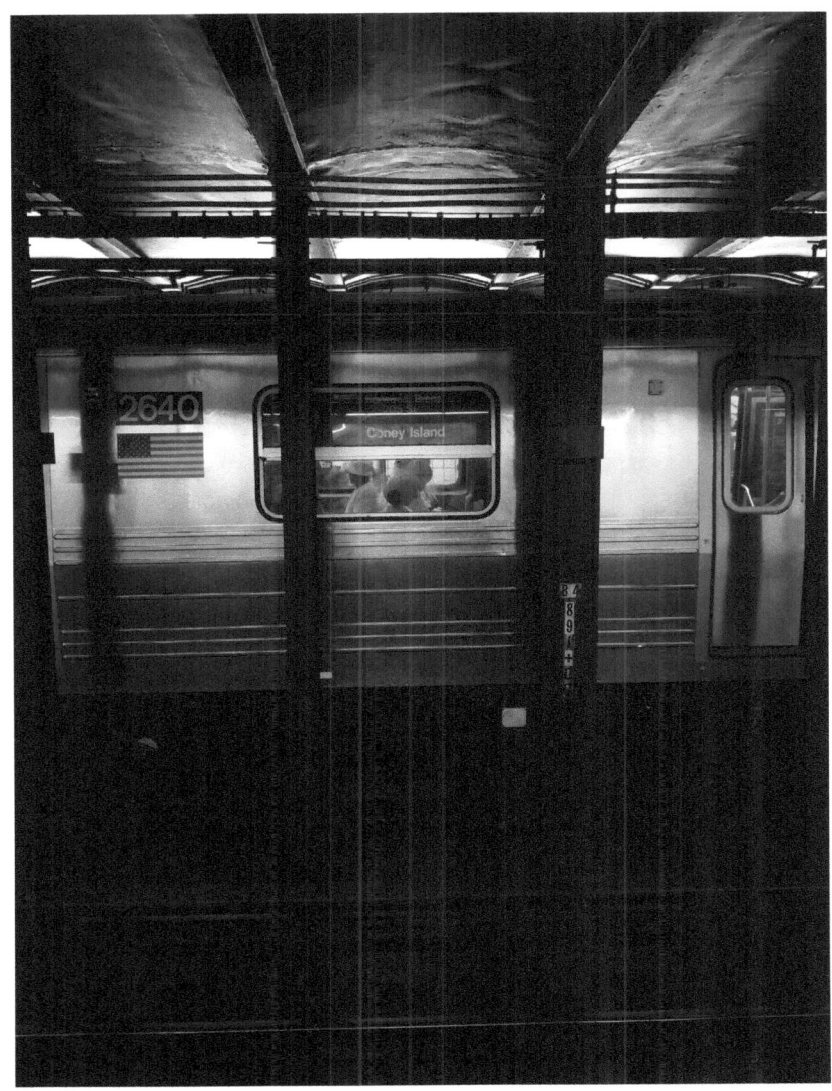

File Name: IMG_20180721_130623.jpg
Date: 07/21/2018 01:06 PM
Width: 3464 pixels
Height: 4618 pixels
Exposure Time: 1/250 sec.
F-stop: f/1.6
ISO: 50
Focal Length: 27mm
GPS Longitude: West
GPS Longitude: -73.993705749444
GPS Latitude: North
GPS Latitude: 40.718158721667

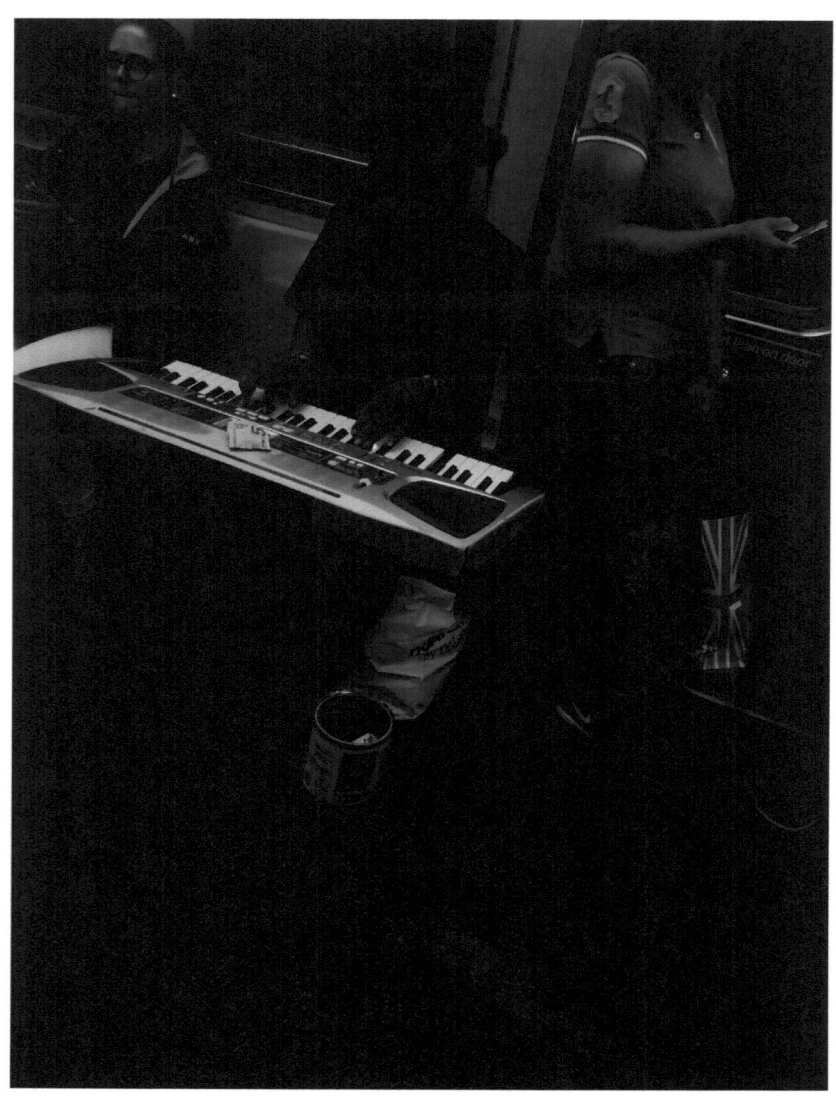

File Name: IMG_20180722_175530.jpg
Date: 07/22/2018 05:55 PM
Width: 3464 pixels
Height: 4618 pixels
Exposure Time: 1/400 sec.
F-stop: f/1.6
ISO: 1600
Focal Length: 27mm
GPS Longitude: West
GPS Longitude: -73.981628417778
GPS Latitude: North
GPS Latitude: 40.768306731944

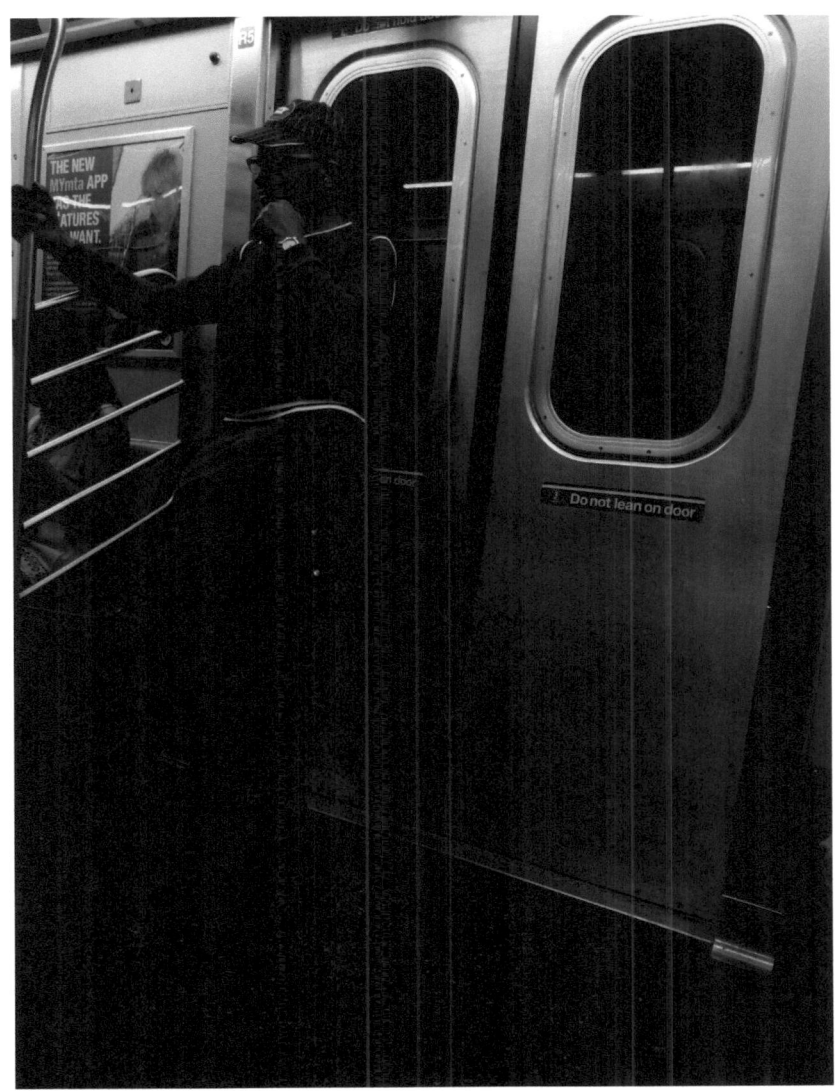

File Name: IMG_20180720_224716.jpg
Date: 07/20/2018 10:47 PM
Width: 3464 pixels
Height: 4618 pixels
Exposure Time: 1/60 sec.
F-stop: f/1.6
ISO: 64
Focal Length: 27mm
GPS Longitude: West
GPS Longitude: Unknown
GPS Latitude: North
GPS Latitude: Unknown

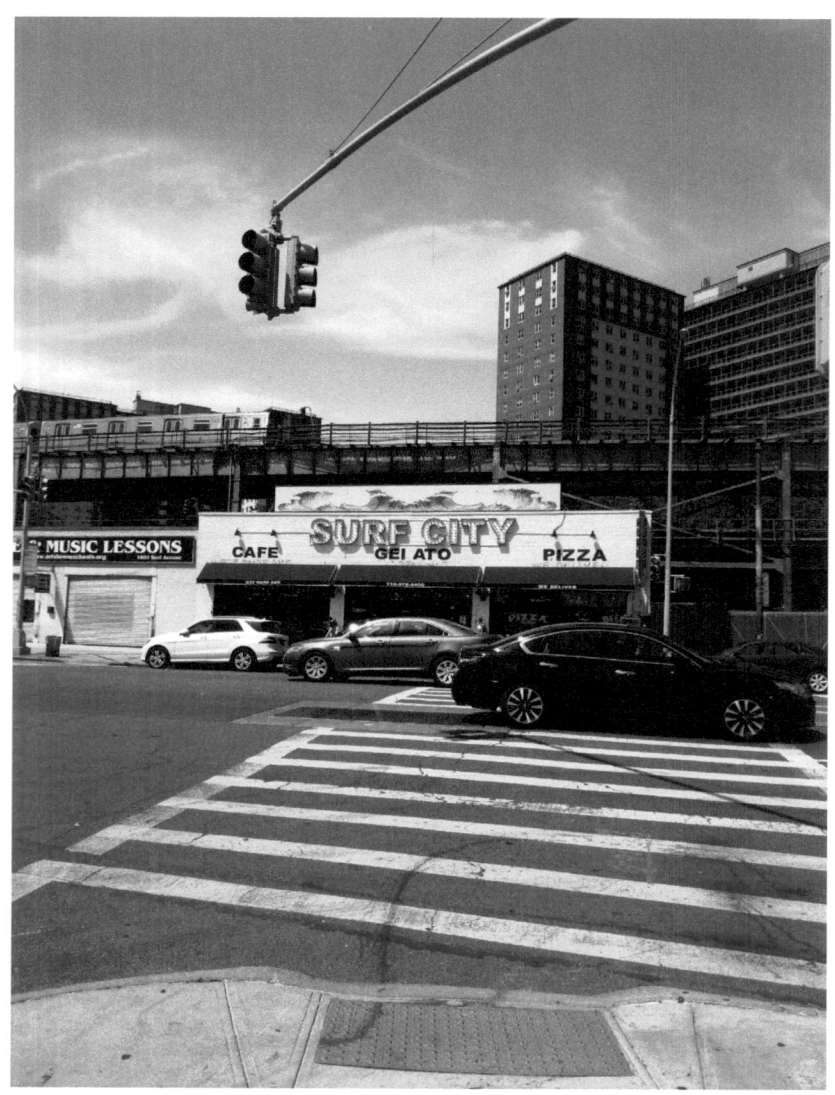

File Name: IMG_20180720_143722.jpg
Date: 07/20/2018 02:37 PM
Width: 3464 pixels
Height: 4618 pixels
Exposure Time: 1/4000 sec.
F-stop: f/1.6
ISO: 64
Focal Length: 27mm
GPS Longitude: West
GPS Longitude: -73.977806091111
GPS Latitude: North
GPS Latitude: 40.5753822325

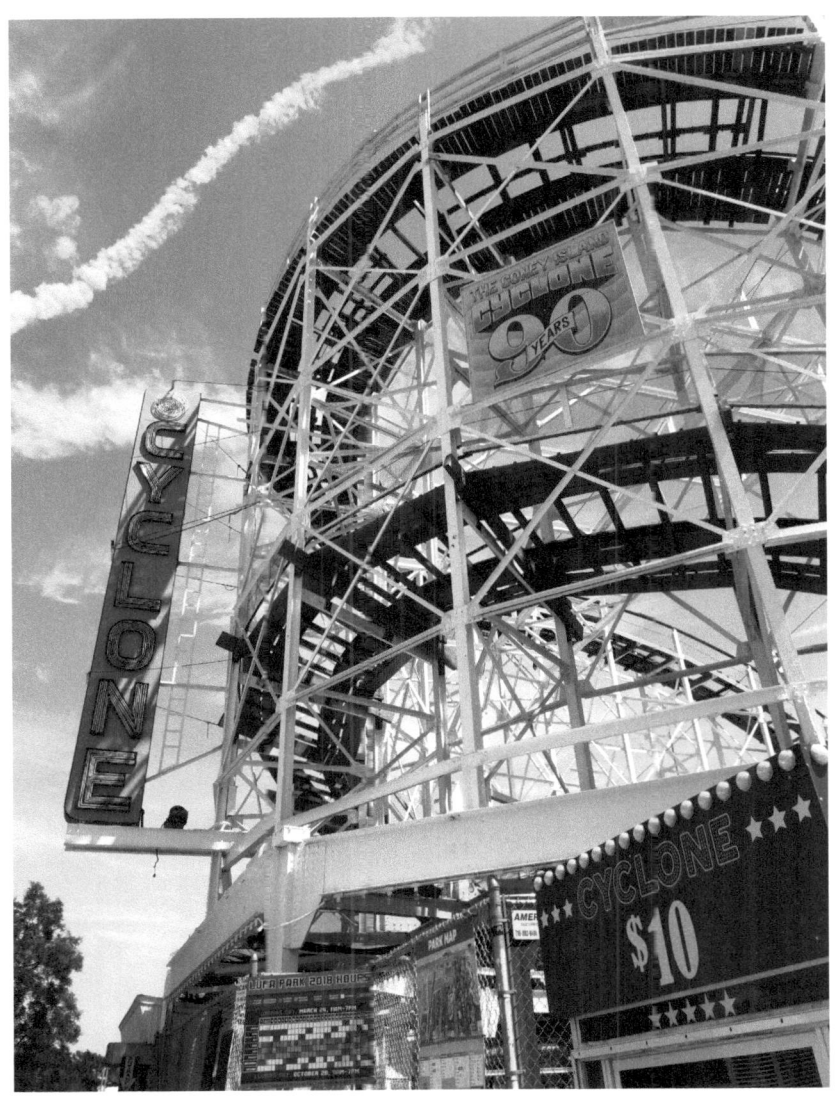

File Name: IMG_20180720_143656.jpg
Date: 07/20/2018 02:36 PM
Width: 3464 pixels
Height: 4618 pixels
Exposure Time: 1/4000 sec.
F-stop: f/1.6
ISO: 64
Focal Length: 27mm
GPS Longitude: West
GPS Longitude: -73.977295753417
GPS Latitude: North
GPS Latitude: 40.574637160371

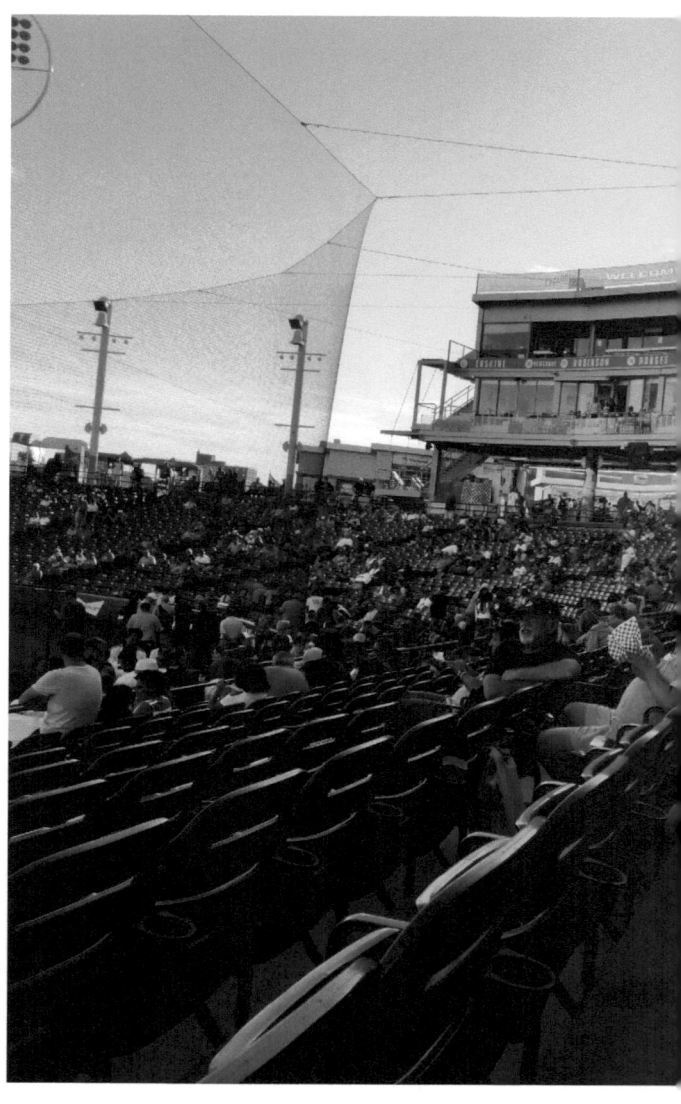

File Name: IMG_20180720_183521.jpg
Date: 07/20/2018 06:35 PM
Width: 4618 pixels
Height: 3464 pixels
Exposure Time: 1/4000 sec.
F-stop: f/1.6
ISO: 100
Focal Length: 27mm
GPS Longitude: West
GPS Longitude: -73.9845326
GPS Latitude: North
GPS Latitude: 40.5747396

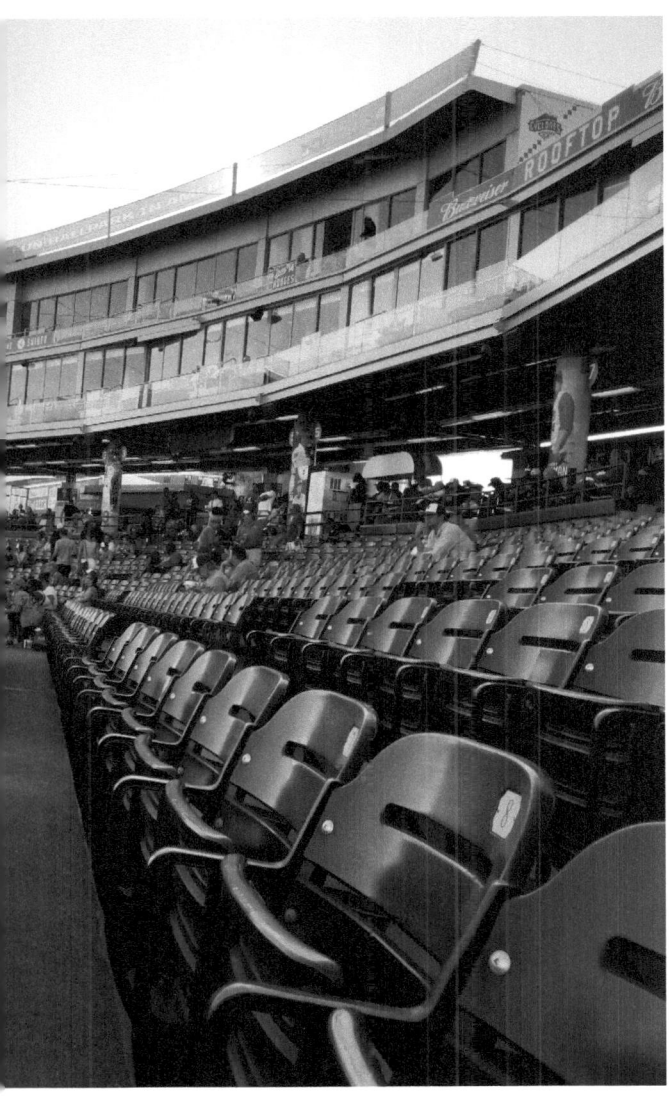

File Name: IMG_20180720_160645.jpg
Date: 07/20/2018 04:06 PM
Width: 3464 pixels
Height: 4618 pixels
Exposure Time: 1/4000 sec.
F-stop: f/1.6
ISO: 50
Focal Length: 27mm
GPS Longitude: West
GPS Longitude: -73.983795165833
GPS Latitude: North
GPS Latitude: 40.571651458611

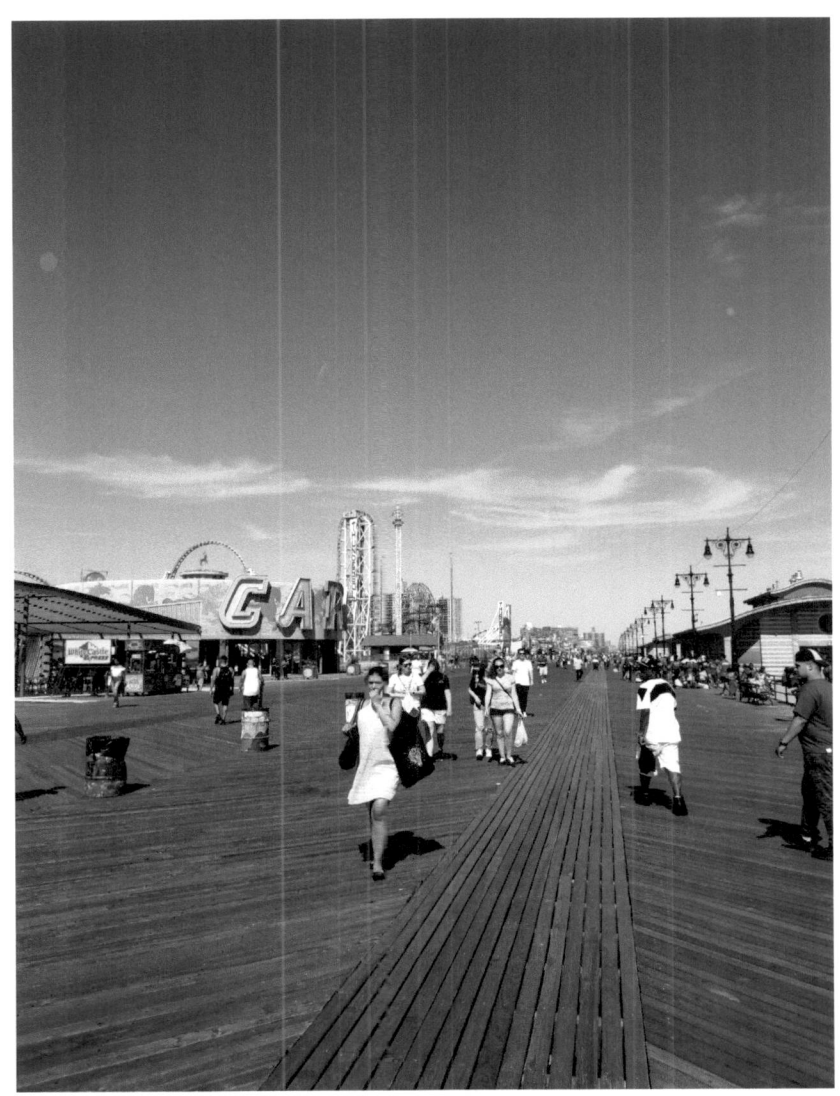

File Name: IMG_20180720_160447.jpg
Date: 07/20/2018 04:04 PM
Width: 3464 pixels
Height: 4618 pixels
Exposure Time: 1/4000 sec.
F-stop: f/1.6
ISO: 50
Focal Length: 27mm
GPS Longitude: West
GPS Longitude: -73.983781088487
GPS Latitude: North
GPS Latitude: 40.572699950688

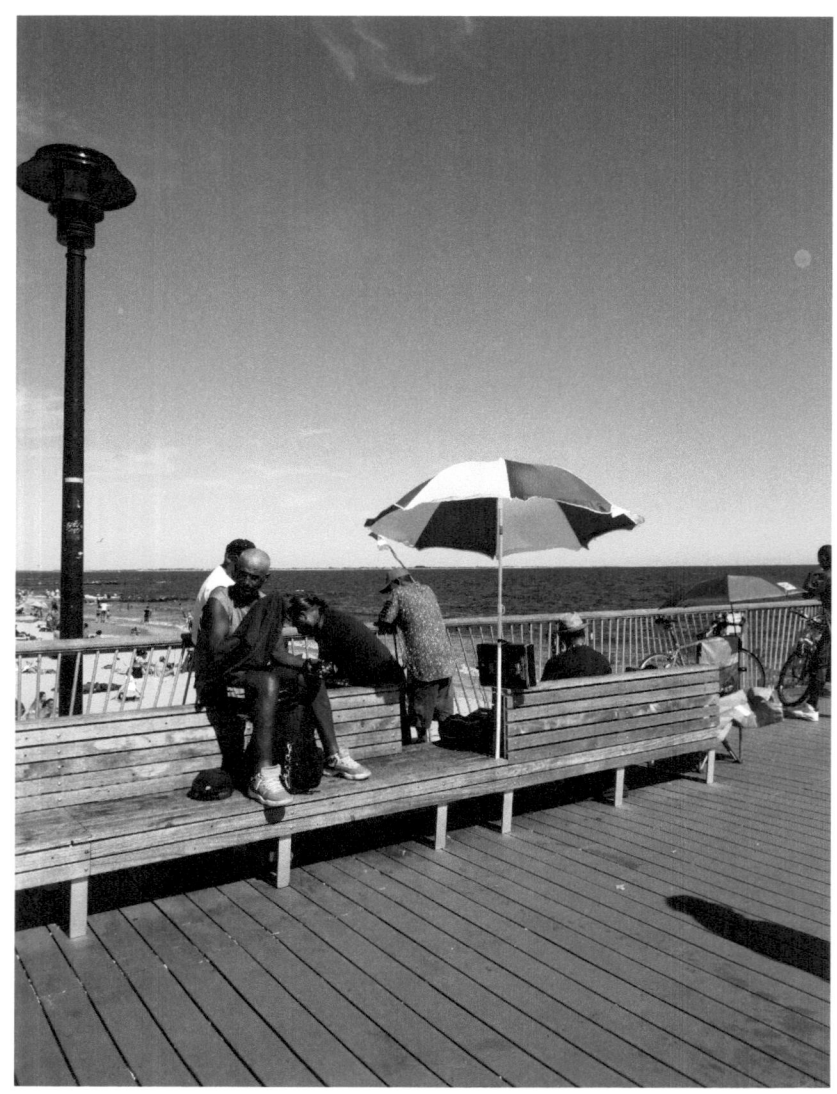

File Name: IMG_20180720_160613.jpg
Date: 07/20/2018 04:06 PM
Width: 3464 pixels
Height: 4618 pixels
Exposure Time: 1/4000 sec.
F-stop: f/1.6
ISO: 50
Focal Length: 27mm
GPS Longitude: West
GPS Longitude: -73.983848571667
GPS Latitude: North
GPS Latitude: 40.5719184875

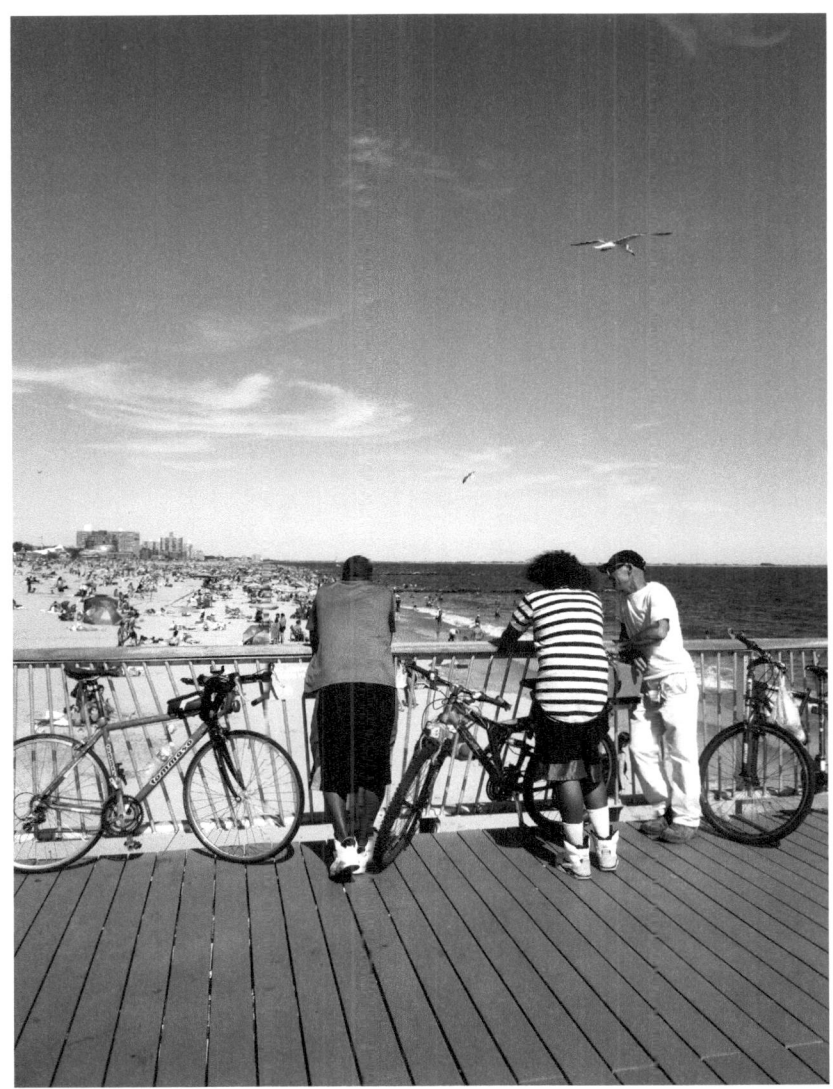

File Name: IMG_20180720_160620.jpg
Date: 07/20/2018 04:06 PM
Width: 3464 pixels
Height: 4618 pixels
Exposure Time: 1/4000 sec.
F-stop: f/1.6
ISO: 50
Focal Length: 27mm
GPS Longitude: West
GPS Longitude: -73.983848571667
GPS Latitude: North
GPS Latitude: 40.5719184875

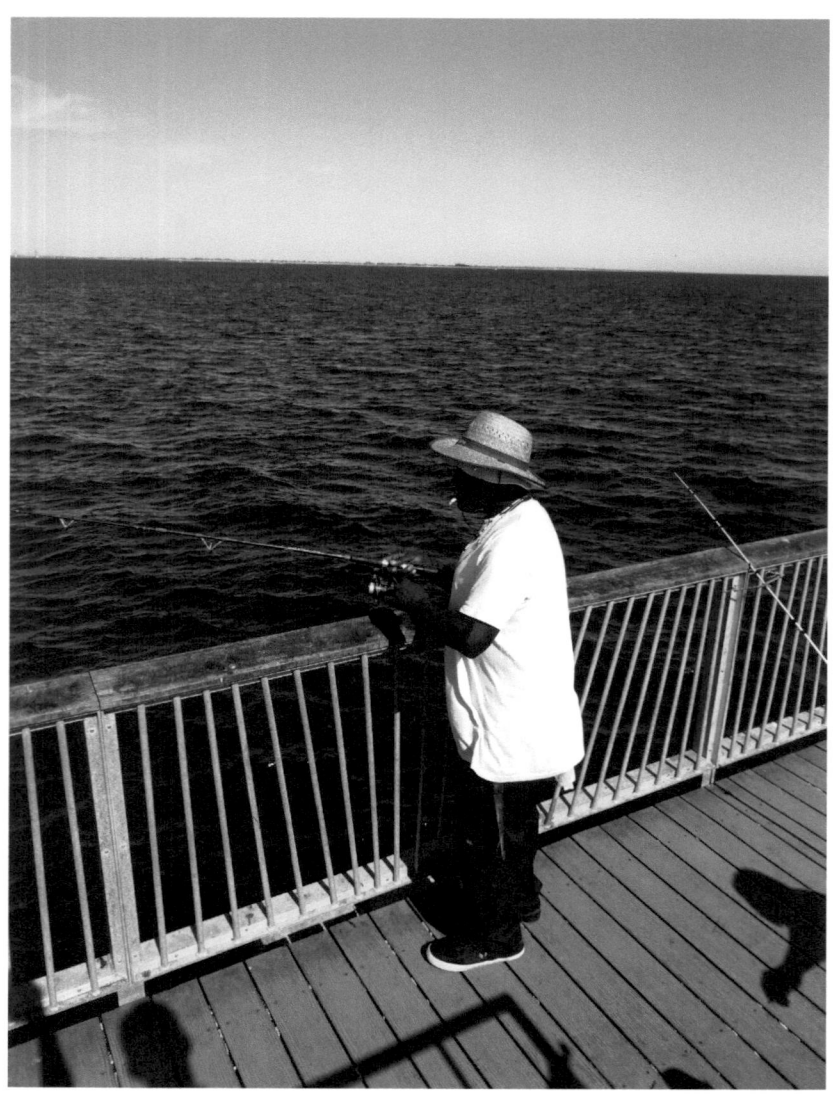

File Name: IMG_20180720_162705.jpg
Date: 07/20/2018 04:27 PM
Width: 3464 pixels
Height: 4618 pixels
Exposure Time: 1/4000 sec.
F-stop: f/1.6
ISO: 50
Focal Length: 27mm
GPS Longitude: West
GPS Longitude: -73.983322143333
GPS Latitude: North
GPS Latitude: 40.569614410278

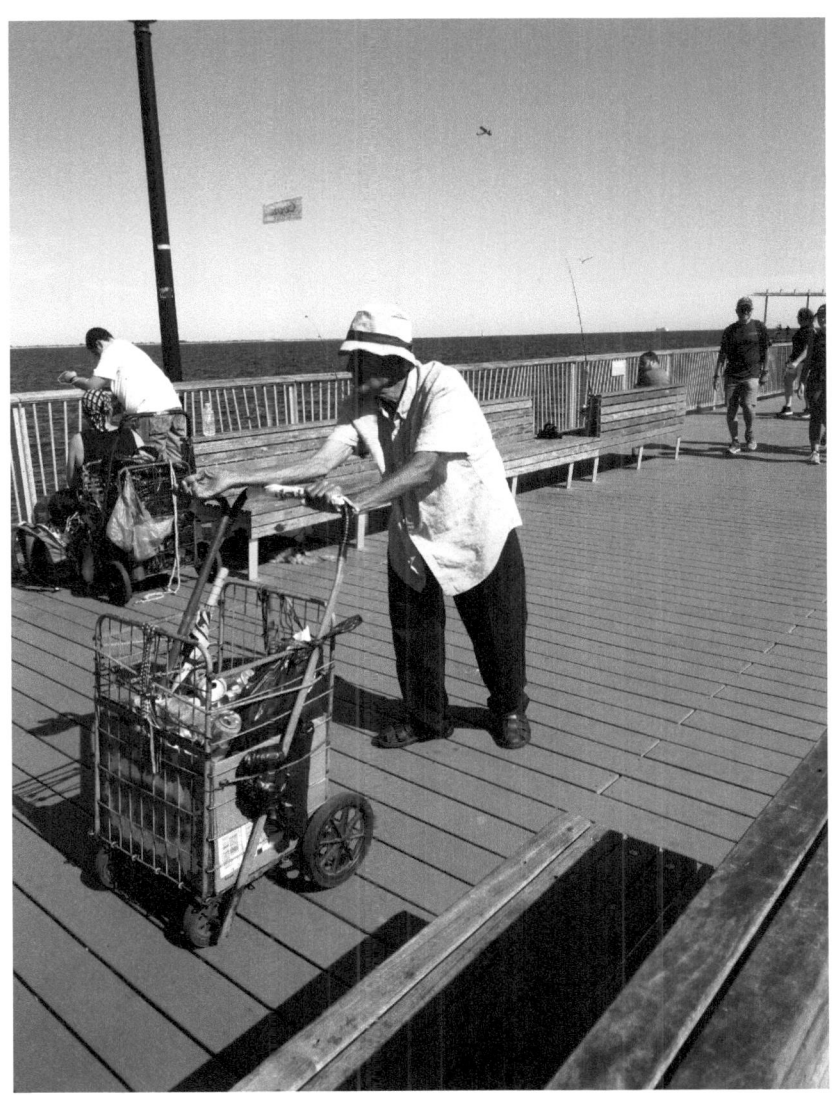

File Name: IMG_20180720_161644.jpg
Date: 07/20/2018 04:16 PM
Width: 3464 pixels
Height: 4618 pixels
Exposure Time: 1/4000 sec.
F-stop: f/1.6
ISO: 50
Focal Length: 27mm
GPS Longitude: West
GPS Longitude: -73.983673095556
GPS Latitude: North
GPS Latitude: 40.571079253889

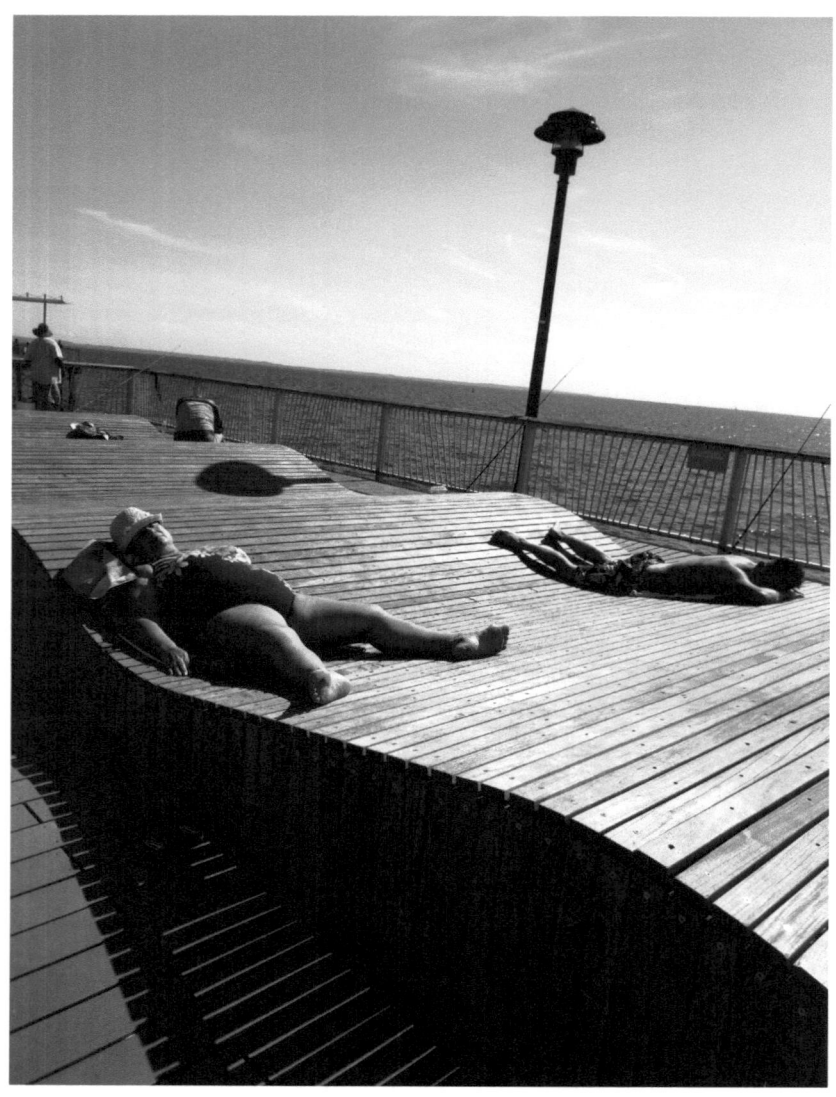

File Name: IMG_20180720_161658.jpg
Date: 07/20/2018 04:16 PM
Width: 3464 pixels
Height: 4618 pixels
Exposure Time: 1/4000 sec.
F-stop: f/1.6
ISO: 50
Focal Length: 27mm
GPS Longitude: West
GPS Longitude: -73.983673095556
GPS Latitude: North
GPS Latitude: 40.571079253889

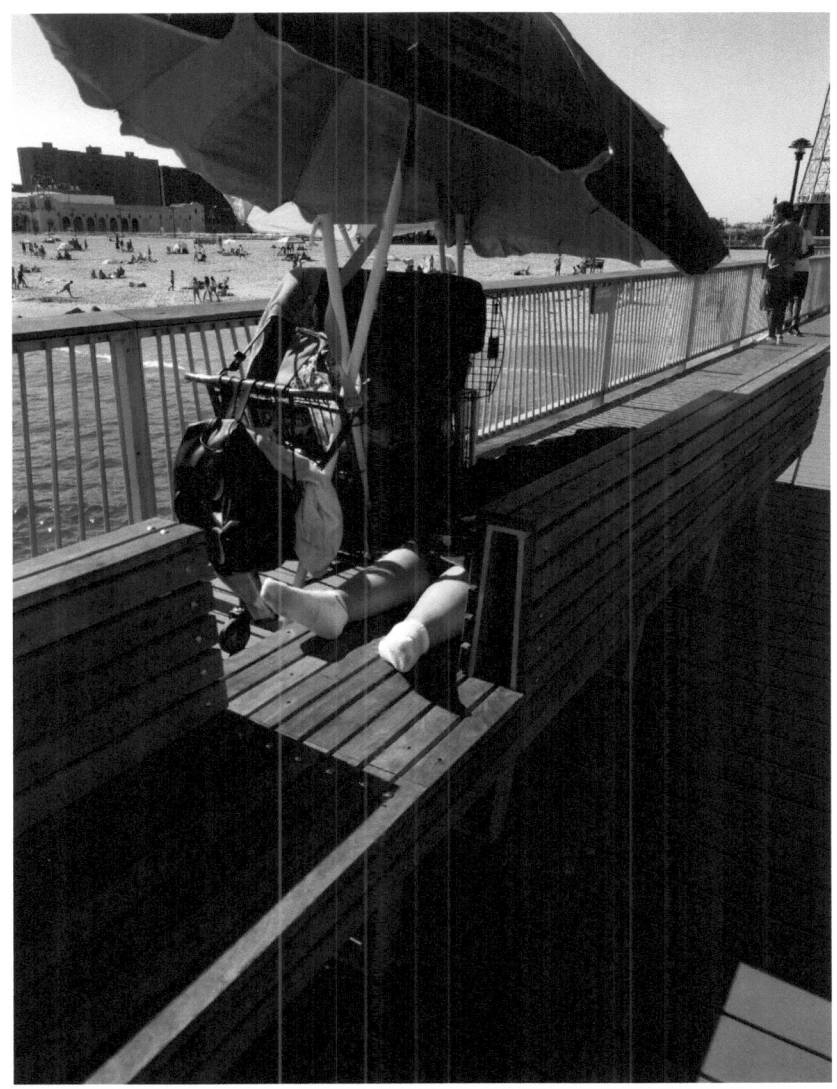

File Name: IMG_20180720_163755.jpg
Date: 07/20/2018 04:37 PM
Width: 3464 pixels
Height: 4618 pixels
Exposure Time: 1/4000 sec.
F-stop: f/1.6
ISO: 50
Focal Length: 27mm
GPS Longitude: West
GPS Longitude: -73.983703613056
GPS Latitude: North
GPS Latitude: 40.571269988889

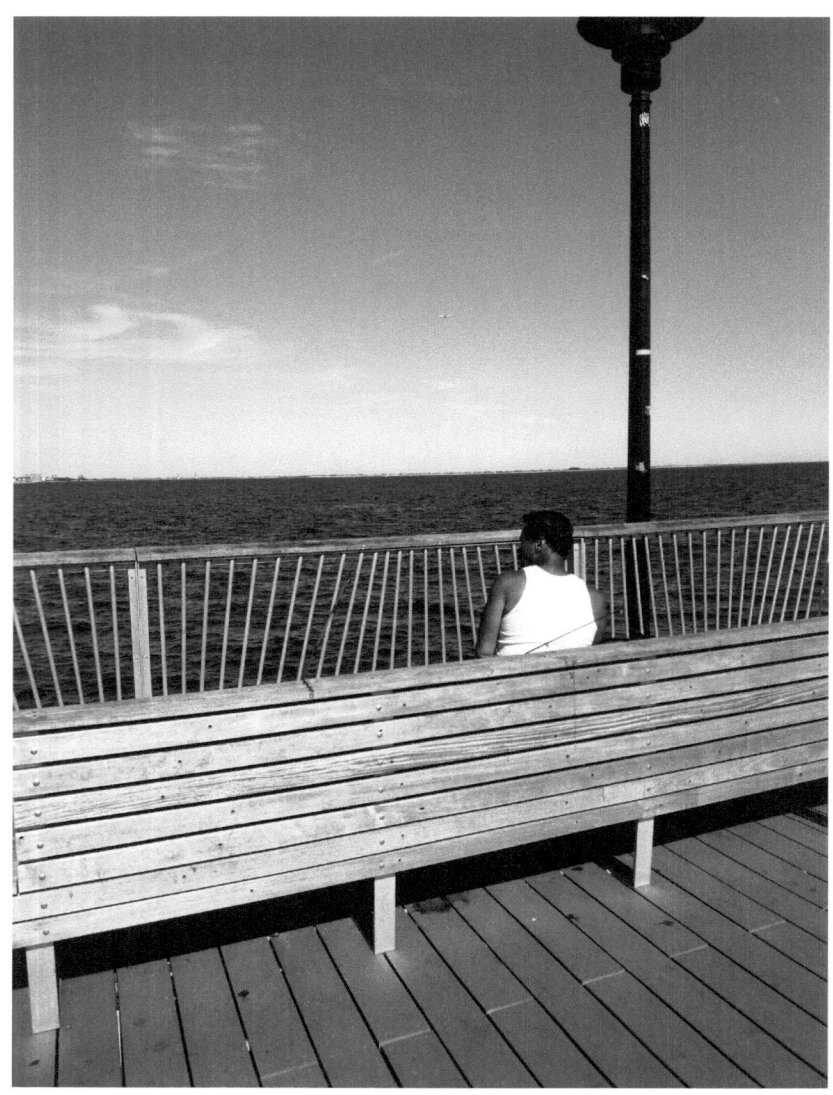

File Name: IMG_20180720_161849.jpg
Date: 07/20/2018 04:18 PM
Width: 3464 pixels
Height: 4618 pixels
Exposure Time: 1/4000 sec.
F-stop: f/1.6
ISO: 50
Focal Length: 27mm
GPS Longitude: West
GPS Longitude: -73.983390808056
GPS Latitude: North
GPS Latitude: 40.569820403889

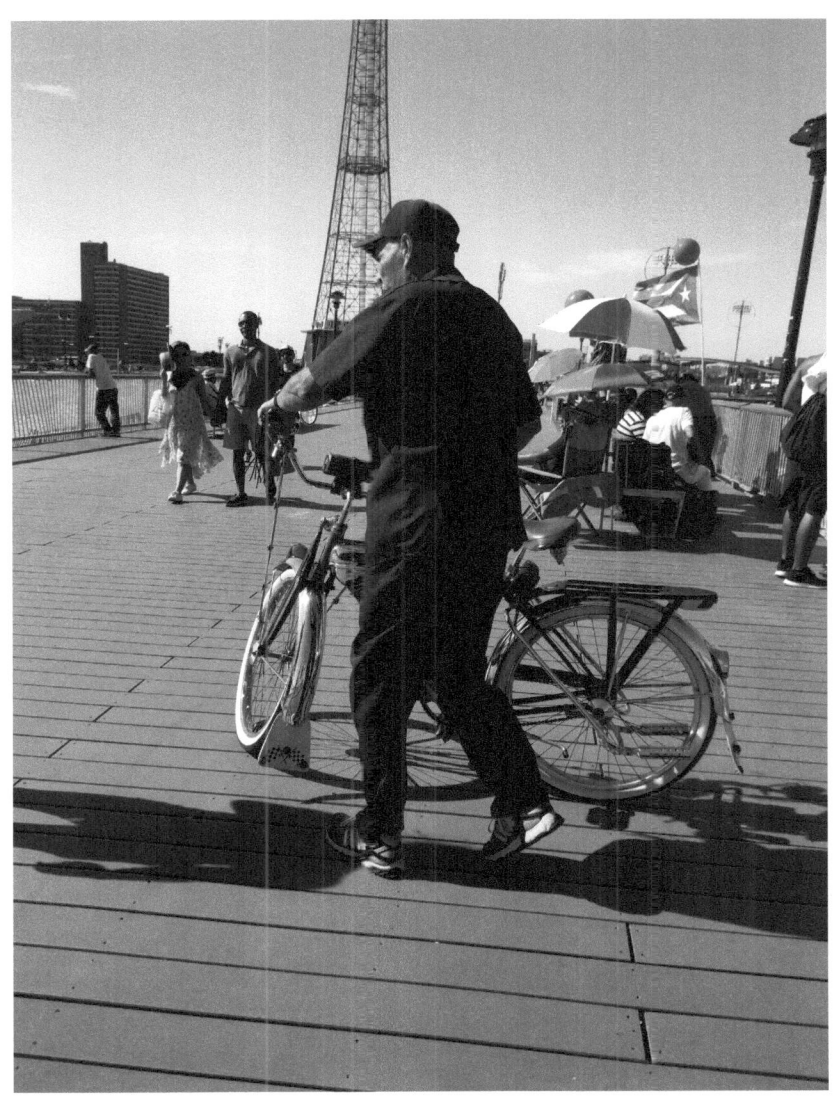

File Name: IMG_20180720_163837.jpg
Date: 07/20/2018 04:38 PM
Width: 3464 pixels
Height: 4618 pixels
Exposure Time: 1/4000 sec.
F-stop: f/1.6
ISO: 50
Focal Length: 27mm
GPS Longitude: West
GPS Longitude: -73.983734130833
GPS Latitude: North
GPS Latitude: 40.571590423333

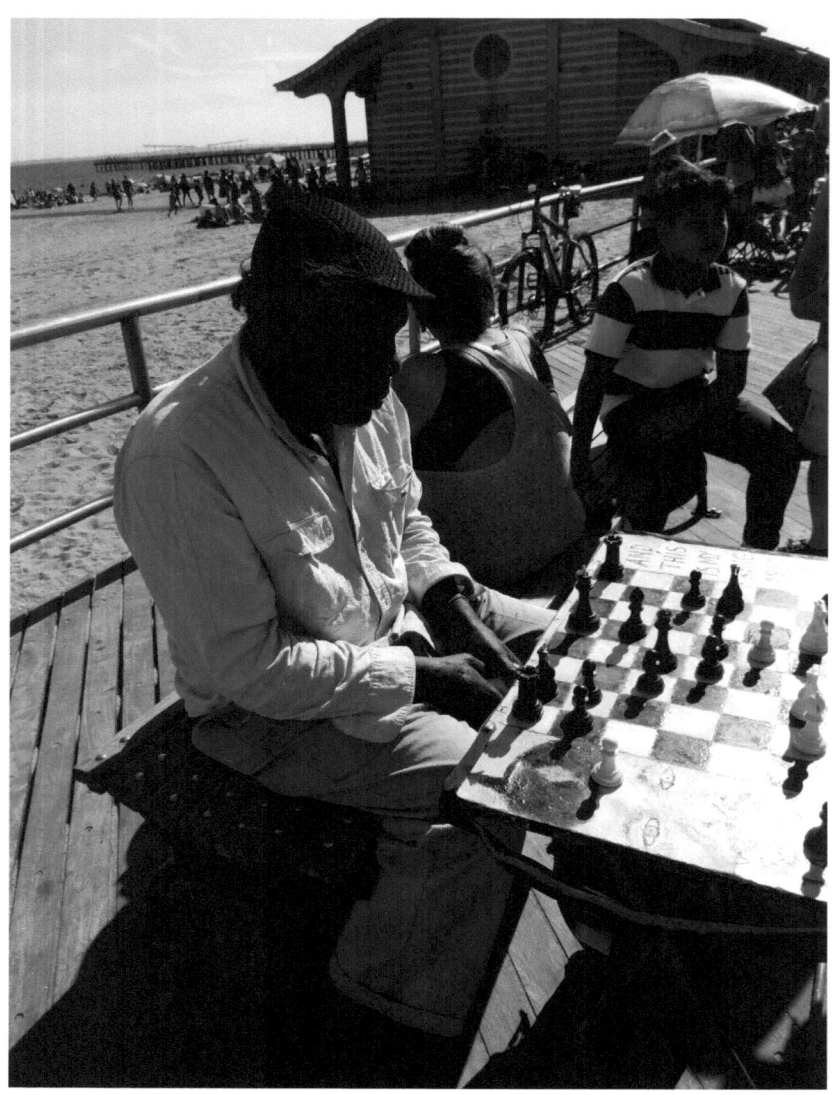

File Name: IMG_20180720_165421.jpg
Date: 07/20/2018 04:54 PM
Width: 3464 pixels
Height: 4618 pixels
Exposure Time: 1/4000 sec.
F-stop: f/1.6
ISO: 50
Focal Length: 27mm
GPS Longitude: West
GPS Longitude: -73.980216979722
GPS Latitude: North
GPS Latitude: 40.573085784722

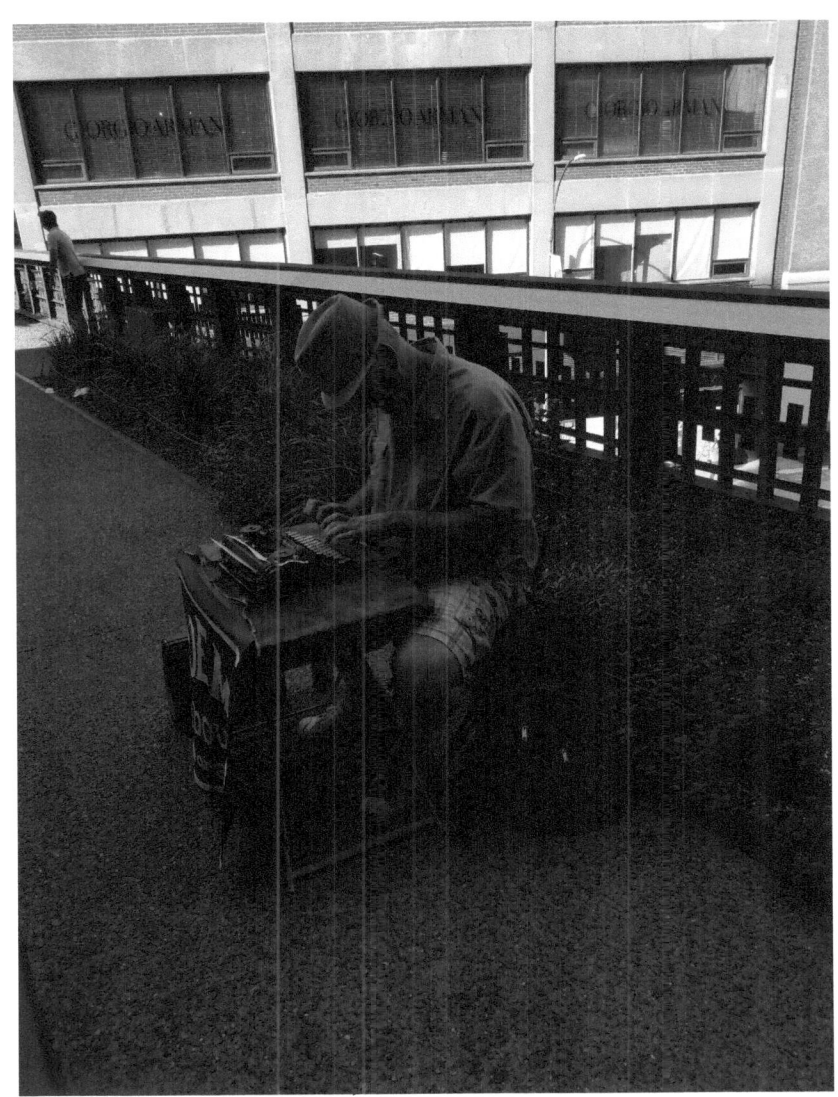

File Name: IMG_20180719_165407.jpg
Date: 07/19/2018 04:54 PM
Width: 3464 pixels
Height: 4618 pixels
Exposure Time: 1/4000 sec.
F-stop: f/1.6
ISO: 125
Focal Length: 27mm
GPS Longitude: West
GPS Longitude: -74.007499694722
GPS Latitude: North
GPS Latitude: 40.742080688333

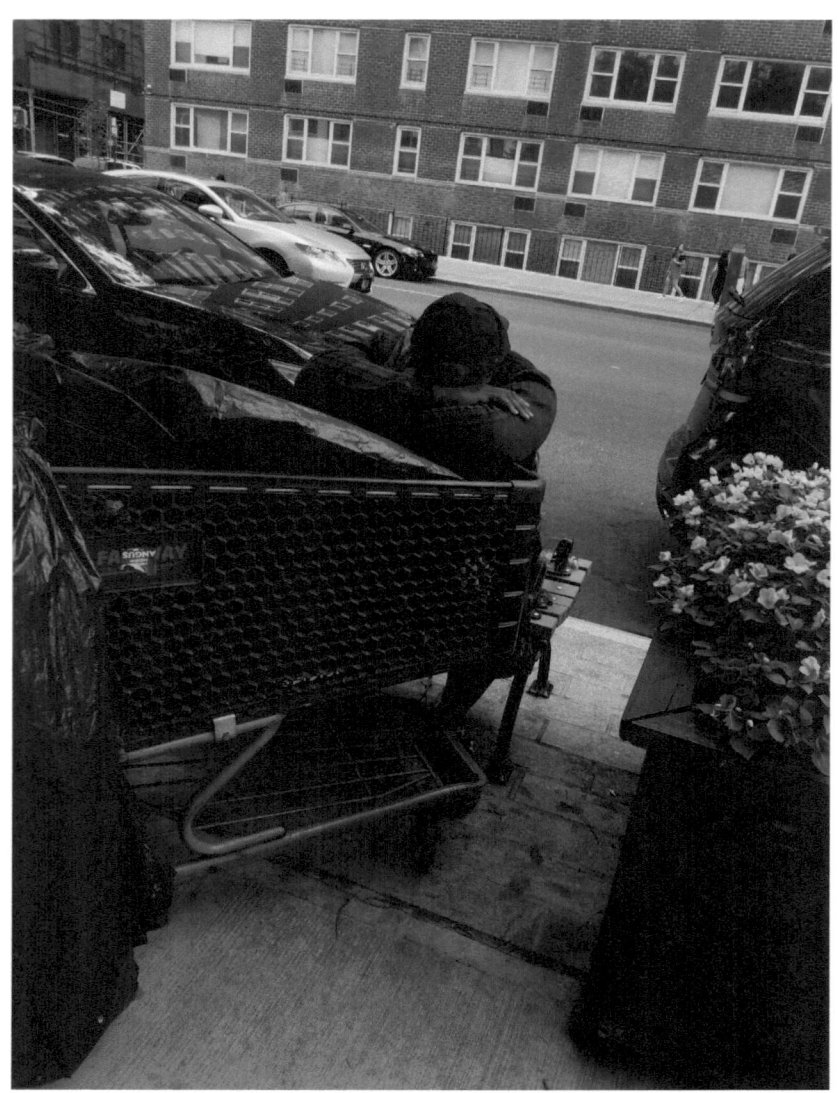

File Name: IMG_20180721_160255.jpg
Date: 07/21/2018 04:02 PM
Width: 3464 pixels
Height: 4618 pixels
Exposure Time: 1/4000 sec.
F-stop: f/1.6
ISO: 125
Focal Length: 27mm
GPS Longitude: West
GPS Longitude: -74.003791808889
GPS Latitude: North
GPS Latitude: 40.726581573333

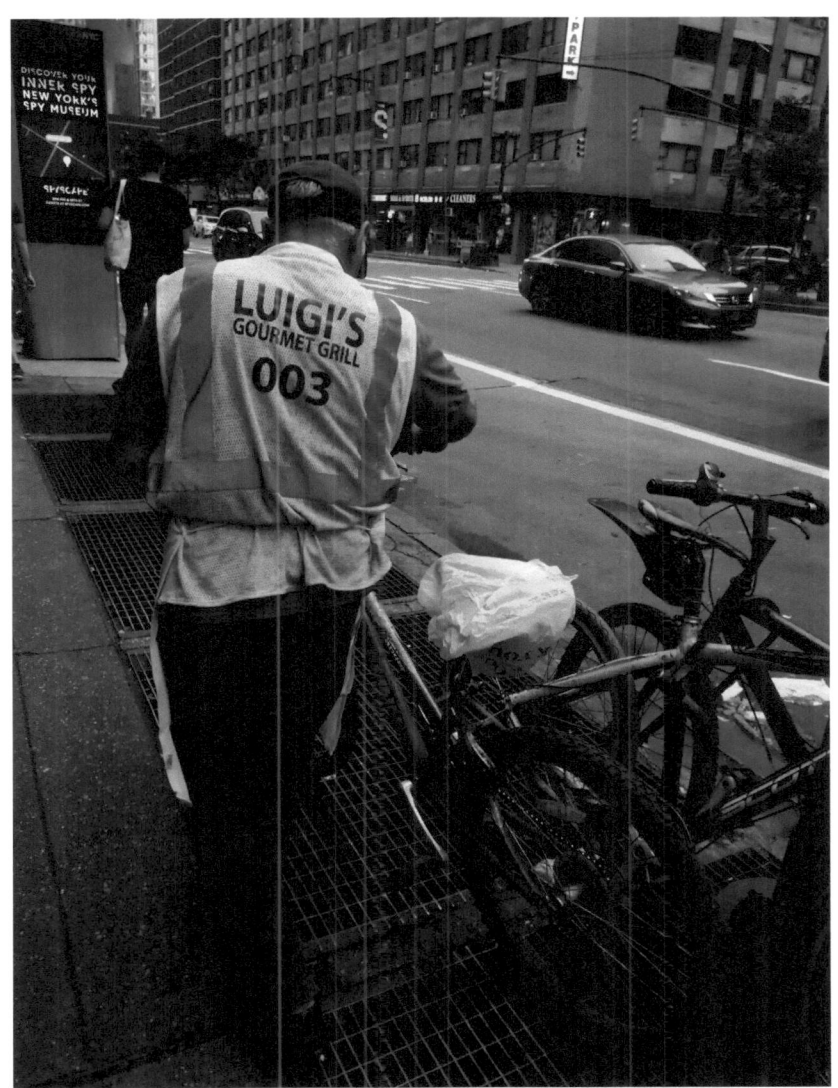

File Name: IMG_20180722_172254.jpg
Date: 07/22/2018 05:22 PM
Width: 3464 pixels
Height: 4618 pixels
Exposure Time: 1/4000 sec.
F-stop: f/1.6
ISO: 1600
Focal Length: 27mm
GPS Longitude: West
GPS Longitude: -73.983726932499
GPS Latitude: North
GPS Latitude: 40.7654634566566

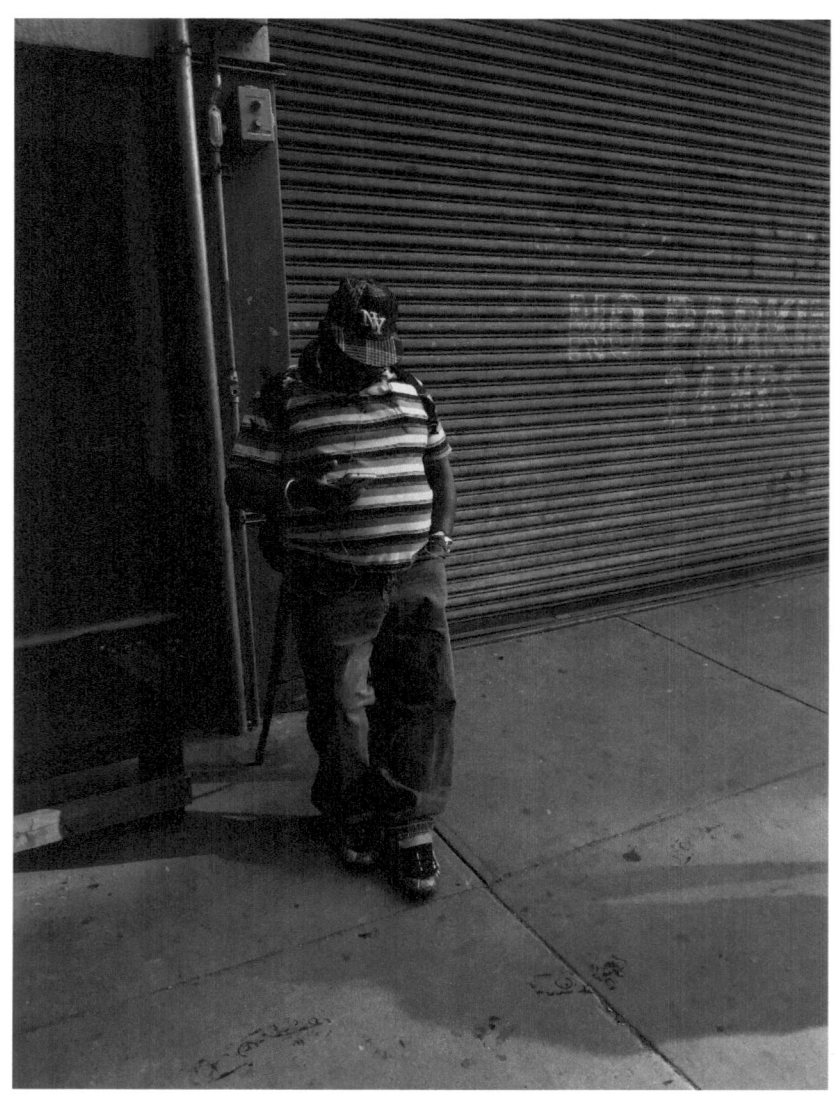

File Name: IMG_20180719_175001.jpg
Date: 07/19/2018 05:50 PM
Width: 3464 pixels
Height: 4618 pixels
Exposure Time: 1/4000 sec.
F-stop: f/1.6
ISO: 200
Focal Length: 27mm
GPS Longitude: West
GPS Longitude: -73.995033263889
GPS Latitude: North
GPS Latitude: 40.761047363056

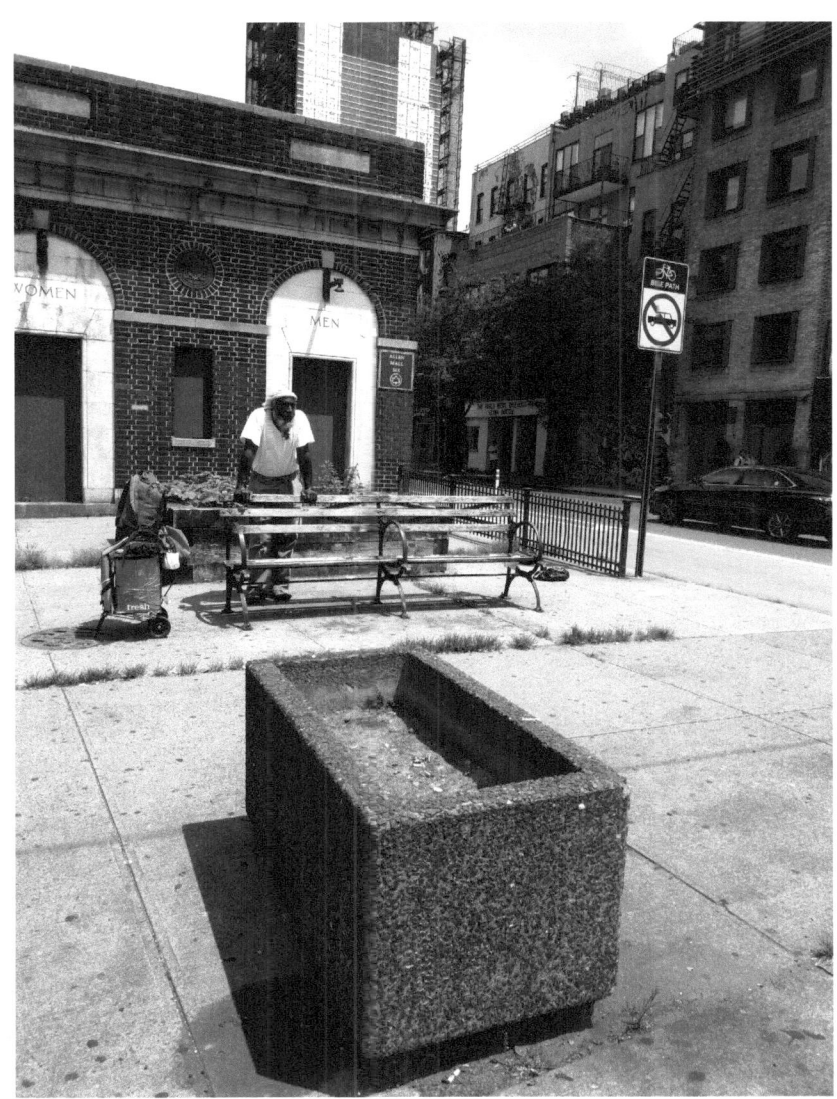

File Name: IMG_20180721_123108.jpg
Date: 07/21/2018 12:31 PM
Width: 3464 pixels
Height: 4618 pixels
Exposure Time: 1/4000 sec.
F-stop: f/1.6
ISO: 80
Focal Length: 27mm
GPS Longitude: West
GPS Longitude: -73.993402302525
GPS Latitude: North
GPS Latitude: 40.750655765930

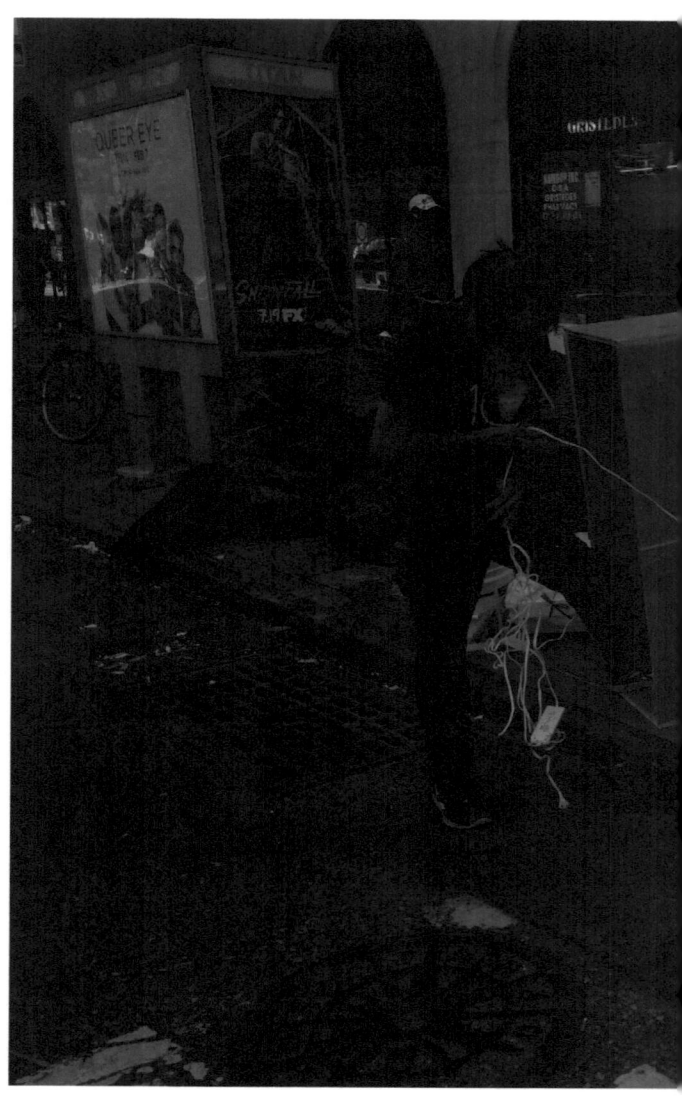

File Name: IMG_20180719_160907.jpg
Date: 07/19/2018 04:09 PM
Width: 4618 pixels
Height: 3464 pixels
Exposure Time: 1/4000 sec.
F-stop: f/1.6
ISO: 100
Focal Length: 27mm
GPS Longitude: West
GPS Longitude: -74.000968933056
GPS Latitude: North
GPS Latitude: 40.747177123889

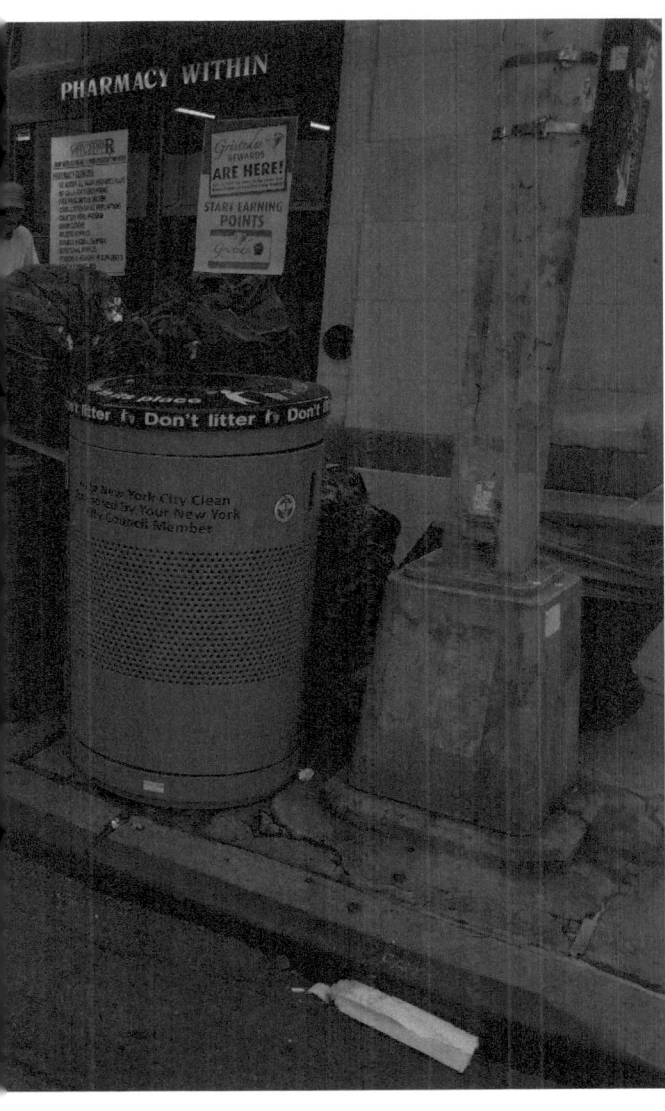

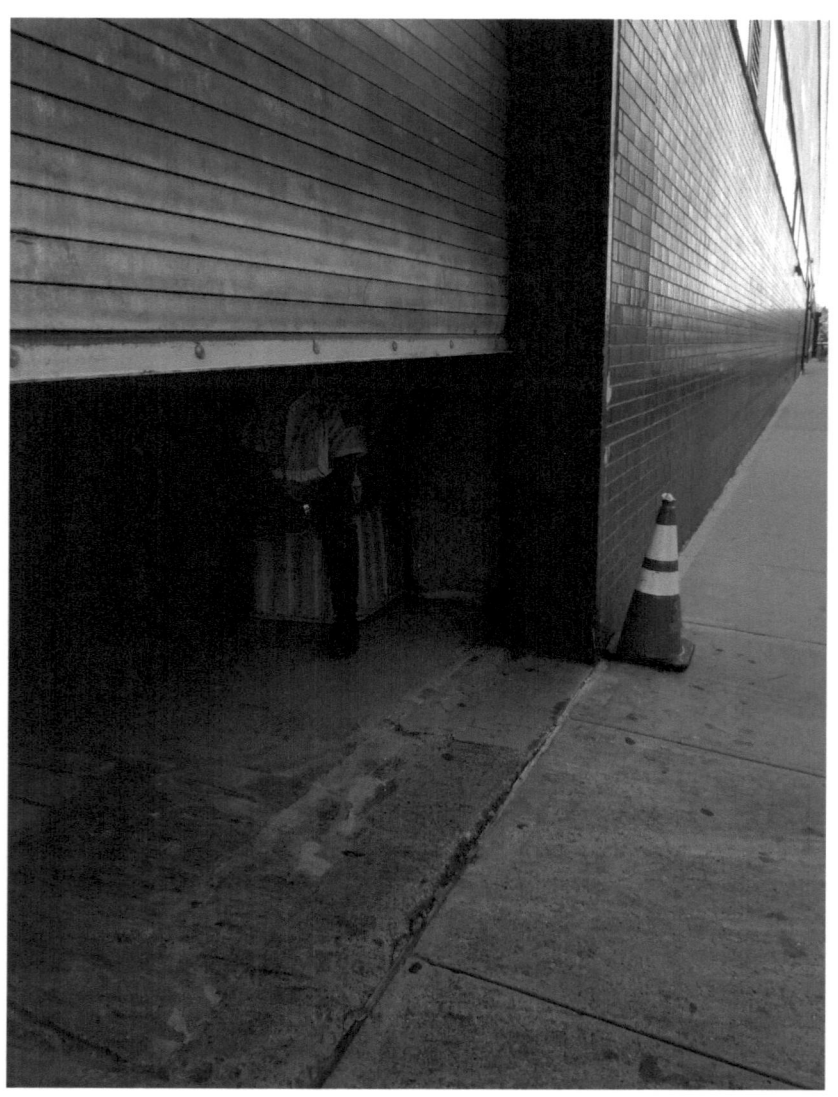

File Name: IMG_20180719_175322.jpg
Date: 07/19/2018 05:53 PM
Width: 3464 pixels
Height: 4618 pixels
Exposure Time: 1/4000 sec.
F-stop: f/1.6
ISO: 250
Focal Length: 27mm
GPS Longitude: West
GPS Longitude: -73.998023986667
GPS Latitude: North
GPS Latitude: 40.762386321944

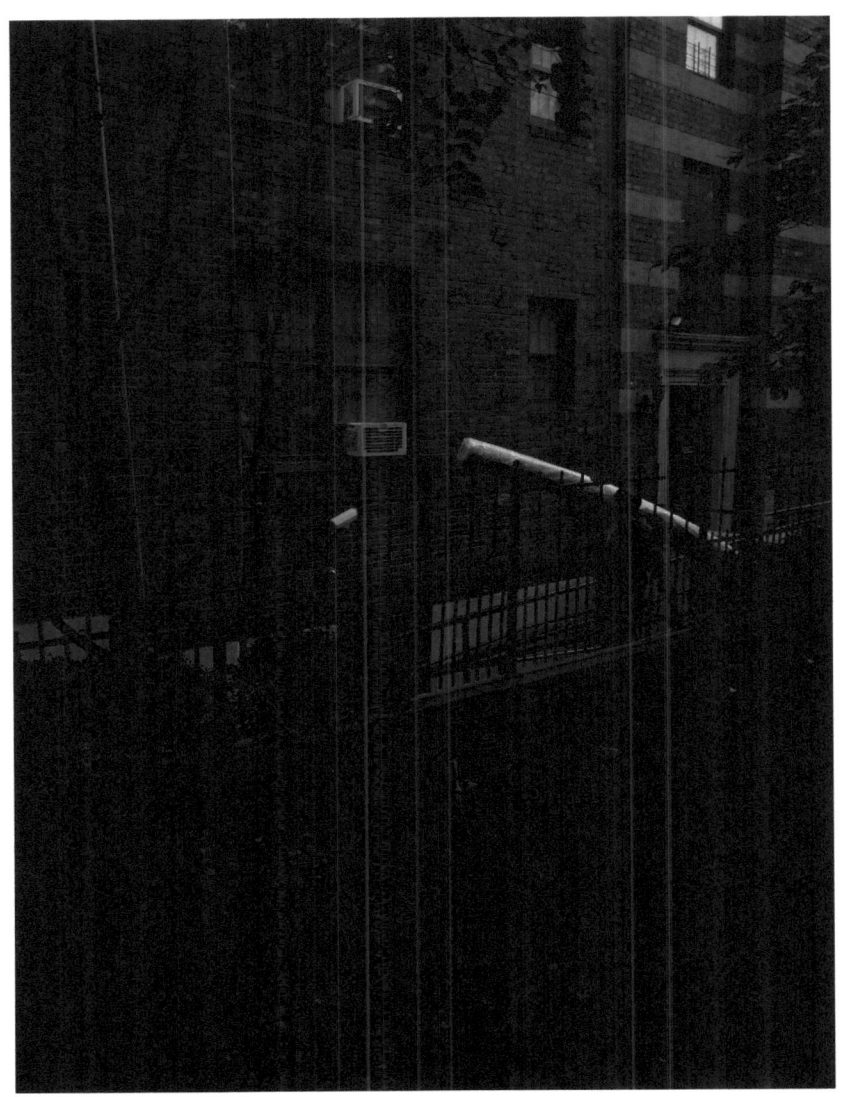

File Name: IMG_20180719_161040.jpg
Date: 07/19/2018 04:10 PM
Width: 3464 pixels
Height: 4618 pixels
Exposure Time: 1/4000 sec.
F-stop: f/1.6
ISO: 500
Focal Length: 27mm
GPS Longitude: West
GPS Longitude: -74.001777648889
GPS Latitude: North
GPS Latitude: 40.747730255

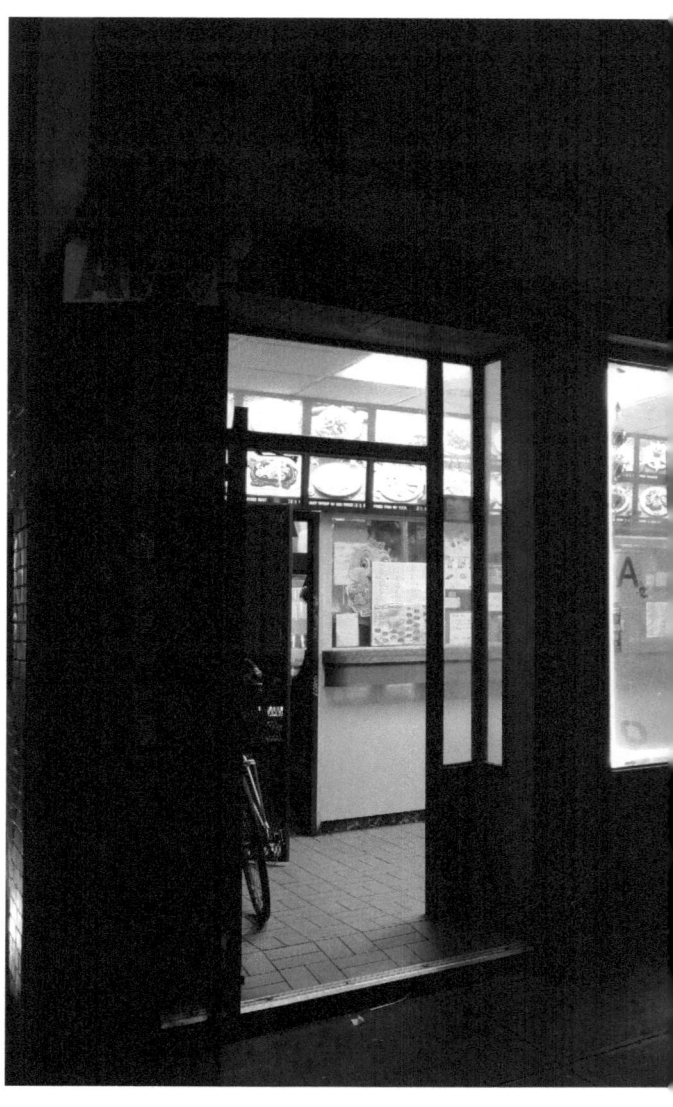

File Name: IMG_20180719_220555.jpg
Date: 07/19/2018 10:05 PM
Width: 4618 pixels
Height: 3464 pixels
Exposure Time: 1/40 sec.
F-stop: f/1.6
ISO: 200
Focal Length: 27mm
GPS Longitude: West
GPS Longitude: Unknown
GPS Latitude: North
GPS Latitude: Unknown

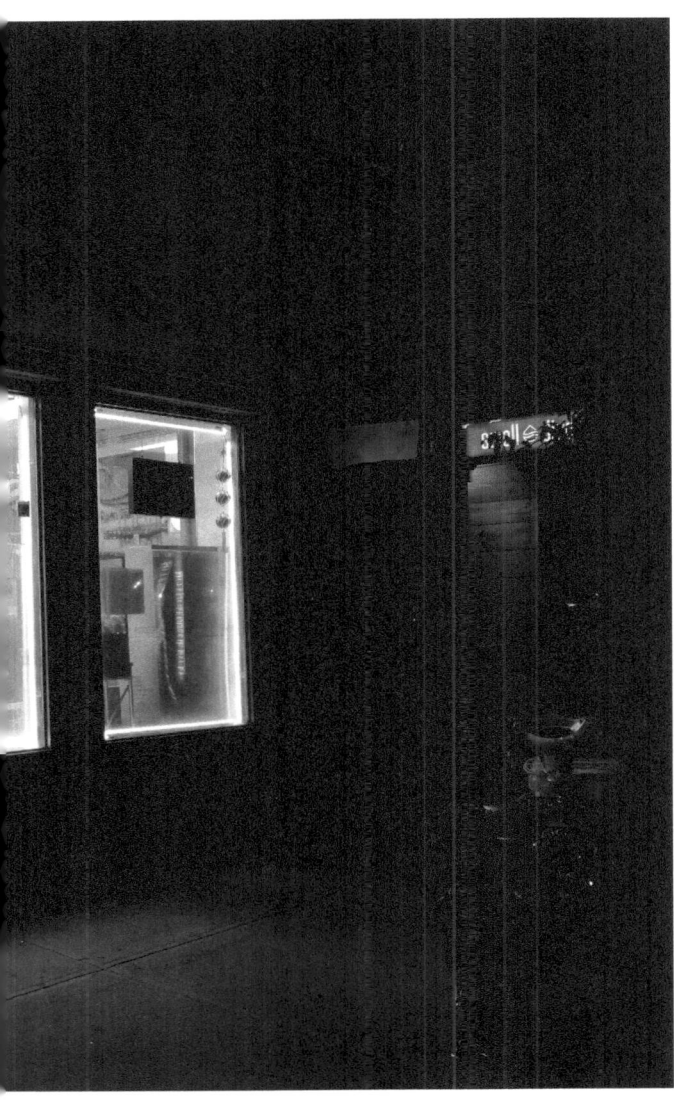

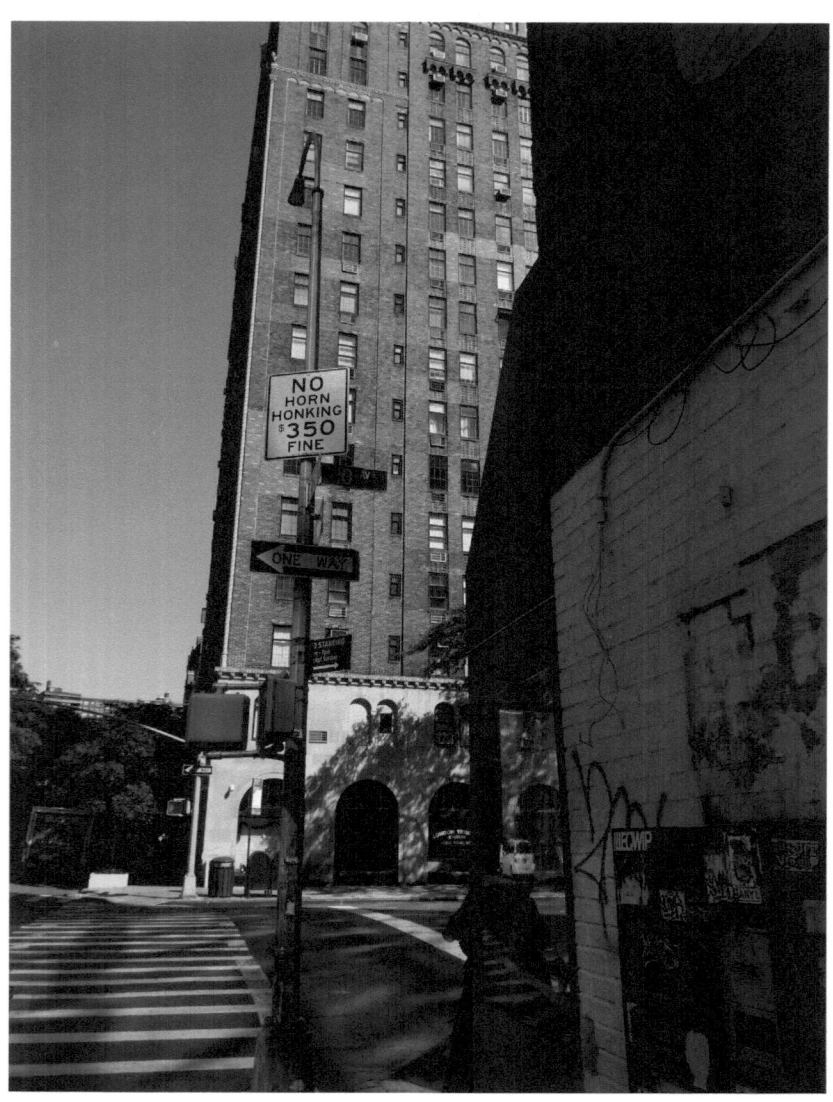

File Name: IMG_20180719_161520.jpg
Date: 07/19/2018 04:15 PM
Width: 3464 pixels
Height: 4618 pixels
Exposure Time: 1/4000 sec.
F-stop: f/1.6
ISO: 50
Focal Length: 27mm
GPS Longitude: West
GPS Longitude: -74.00440979
GPS Latitude: North
GPS Latitude: 40.748485565

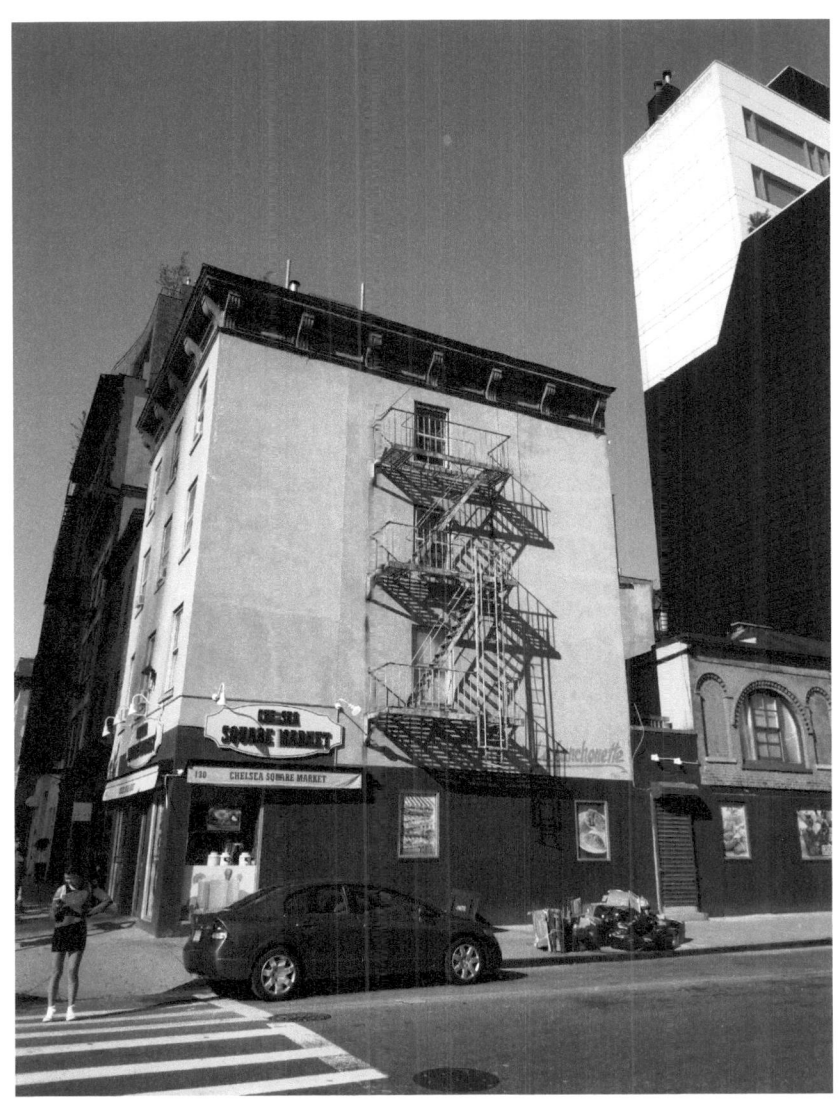

File Name: IMG_20180719_171940.jpg
Date: 07/19/2018 05:19 PM
Width: 3464 pixels
Height: 4618 pixels
Exposure Time: 1/4000 sec.
F-stop: f/1.6
ISO: 50
Focal Length: 27mm
GPS Longitude: West
GPS Longitude: -74.006370544167
GPS Latitude: North
GPS Latitude: 40.744510650556

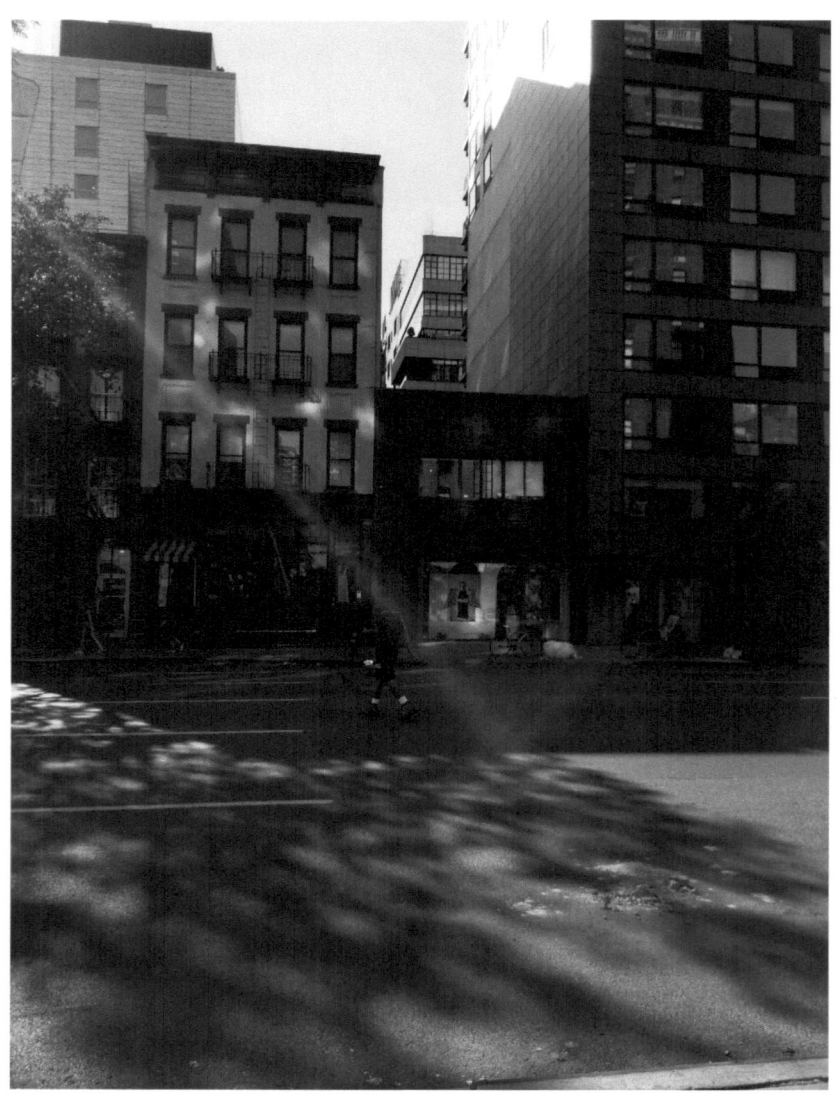

File Name: IMG_20180719_172556.jpg
Date: 07/19/2018 05:25 PM
Width: 3464 pixels
Height: 4618 pixels
Exposure Time: 1/4000 sec.
F-stop: f/1.6
ISO: 50
Focal Length: 27mm
GPS Longitude: West
GPS Longitude: -74.004096984722
GPS Latitude: North
GPS Latitude: 40.747924804444

File Name: IMG_20180719_161646.jpg
Date: 07/19/2018 04:16 PM
Width: 3464 pixels
Height: 4618 pixels
Exposure Time: 1/4000 sec.
F-stop: f/1.6
ISO: 50
Focal Length: 27mm
GPS Longitude: West
GPS Longitude: -74.004470825
GPS Latitude: North
GPS Latitude: 40.748340606667

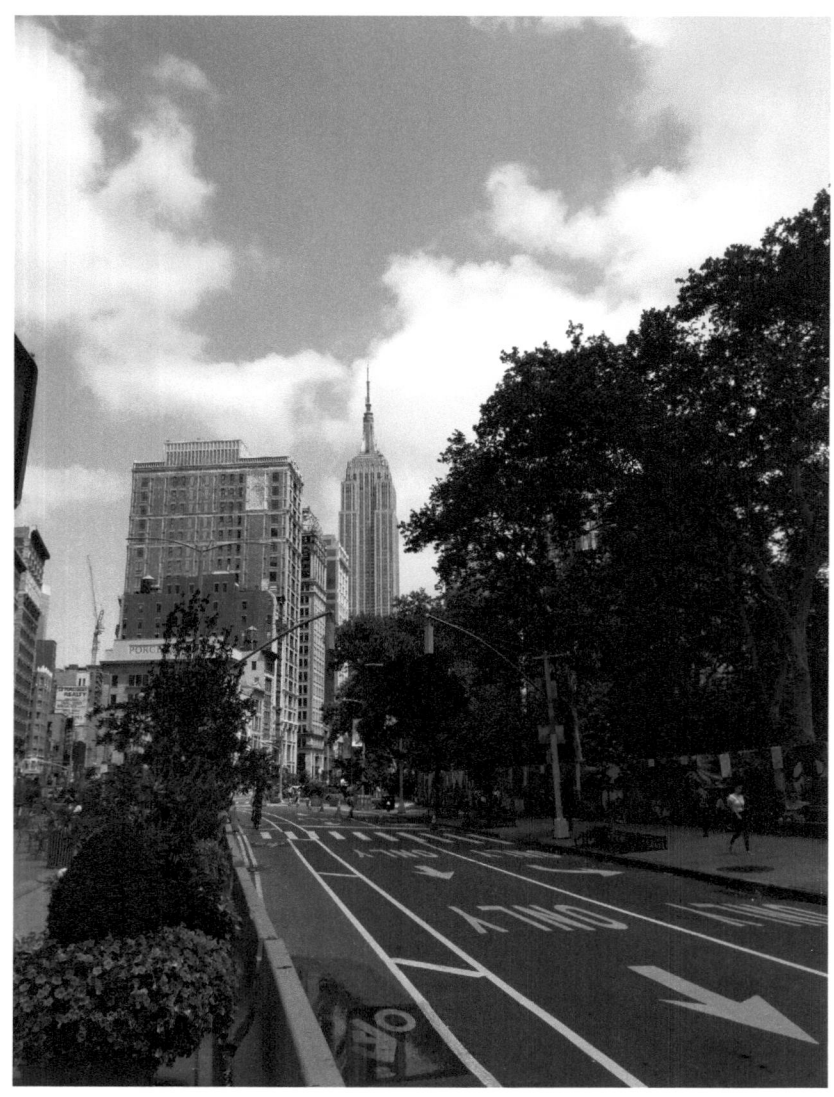

File Name: IMG_20180722_121509.jpg
Date: 07/22/2018 12:15 PM
Width: 3464 pixels
Height: 4618 pixels
Exposure Time: 1/4000 sec.
F-stop: f/1.6
ISO: 50
Focal Length: 27mm
GPS Longitude: West
GPS Longitude: -73.9858499
GPS Latitude: North
GPS Latitude: 40.7604332

www.ingramcontent.com/pod-product-compliance
Lightning Source LLC
Chambersburg PA
CBHW040333220526
45473CB00009B/2667